Prophetic

for 2020 Words

DESTINY IMAGE BOOKS BY LARRY SPARKS

The Glory Has Come

Accessing the Greater Glory

Prophetic Words for 2019

Arise

Ask for the Rain

The Fire that Never Sleeps

Breakthrough Faith

Breakthrough Healing

Prophetic
for 2020 Words

with contributions from...

Emma Stark, Jeremiah Johnson, Lana Vawser,
Robert Henderson, David Balestri, Ana Werner,
Hank and Brenda Kunneman, Patricia King,
Sarah Cheesman, Mario Murillo, Katherine
Ruonala, Rick Joyner, Arleen Westerhof, Gene
Bailey, Kevin Zadai, Betty King, and James Goll

Compiled *by* Larry Sparks

DESTINY IMAGE® PUBLISHERS, INC.

P.O. Box 310, Shippensburg, PA 17257-0310

"Promoting Inspired Lives."

This book and all other Destiny Image and Destiny Image Fiction books are available at Christian bookstores and distributors worldwide.

Cover design by Eileen Rockwell
Interior design by Terry Clifton

For more information on foreign distributors, call 717-532-3040.

Reach us on the Internet: www.destinyimage.com.

ISBN 13 TP: 978-0-7684-5223-5
ISBN 13 eBook: 978-0-7684-5224-2
ISBN 13 HC: 978-0-7684-5226-6
ISBN 13 LP: 978-0-7684-5225-9

For Worldwide Distribution, Printed in the U.S.A.

2 3 4 5 6 7 8 / 24 23 22 21 20

Contents

INTRODUCTION
1

CHAPTER 1

FIVE WAYS THE DEVIL IS TRYING TO
TURN CHRISTIANITY UPSIDE DOWN
by Larry Sparks
5

CHAPTER 2

THE BEGINNING OF THE DAYS OF HOLY POWER
by Emma Stark
17

CHAPTER 3

PROPHETIC ACCURACY, JEALOUSY,
AND POLITICAL TURMOIL
by Jeremiah Johnson
31

CHAPTER 4

2020: THE YEAR OF BOLD FAITH
by Lana Vawser
37

CHAPTER 5

JUSTICE AND UPGRADES: REPLACING THE
INFERIOR WITH THE SUPERIOR
by Robert Henderson
49

CHAPTER 6

THE CHRIST-CONFIGURED CHURCH
AND THE DEMONIAC NATIONS
by David Balestri
59

Chapter 7

A Time of Purification and Pieces Coming Together

by Ana Werner

69

Chapter 8

The Decade of Difference

by Hank and Brenda Kunneman

79

Chapter 9

The Days of Elijah

by Patricia King

87

Chapter 10

Pacesetters, Arise!

by Sarah Cheesman

99

Chapter 11

2020: The Year of Extravagant Asking

by Mario Murillo

109

Chapter 12

The Decade of Declaration and Acceleration

by Katherine Ruonala

119

Chapter 13

Civil War, Revolutionary War, Heaven's Perspective on America, and the Release of Champions

by Rick Joyner

131

CHAPTER 14

2020–2029: THE ERA OF THE NATIONS
by Arleen Westerhof
139

CHAPTER 15

THE RUMBLE OF CULTURE-SHAKING REVIVAL AND AWAKENING
by Gene Bailey
149

CHAPTER 16

THE YEAR OF PERFECT VISION AND 11 DISTINCTIVES OF THE NEXT MOVE OF GOD
by Kevin L. Zadai
157

CHAPTER 17

INTIMACY WITH GOD, DIVINE ALIGNMENTS, AND FRUITFULNESS
by Rev. Betty King
167

CHAPTER 18

A TIME OF GENERATIONAL PROPHETIC INHERITANCE
by James W. Goll
177

CHAPTER 19

A VISION OF THE UNIFIED CHURCH AND THE THIRD MISSING MOVE OF GOD
by Larry Sparks
187

INTRODUCTION

by Larry Sparks

*"Prophetic words are often an
invitation, not an inevitability."*
—KATHERINE RUONALA

We receive this collection of prophetic words with discernment and then we participate with them through our prayer and obedience. I'll never forget a very open, honest conversation I had with my pastor and spiritual father about my concerns with prophetic words that had not come to pass. I was venting my frustration over "all of those prophetic words that are released year after year...but never come to pass." The Lord corrected me by offering a profound, revelatory response.

He said, "The prophets will prophesy." Simple, right? The truth is this: Prophets will continue to prophesy what sound like the same prophetic words, often year after year, *until* someone on the Earth decides to pray, act, and build like that prophetic word is indeed true.

Again, I encourage you to remember while reading through these words that they require your participation. Yes, God is sovereign and He can do what He wants. There *are* prophetic inevitabilities—things Scripture has announced that will come to pass regardless of mankind's involvement. One such inevitability is the second coming of Jesus. Our unique opinions or differing eschatology viewpoints (theology of the end times) will not change whether or not the Lord physically and visibly returns and sets very real and literal feet upon the Mount of Olives in Jerusalem. He's coming back. Period, end of story. And yet, even worked into the sovereign unfolding story of Jesus' return is this very interesting comment from the apostle Peter: *"waiting for and hastening the coming of the day of God"* (2 Pet. 3:12). Yes, the second coming of Jesus is a prophetic inevitability, but reviewing Peter's language here, it seems like it can also be influenced—hastened—by our activity on the Earth.

I will leave the specifics of the prophetic inevitabilities to the Lord. In the meantime, as we live and breathe here on planet Earth, I want us to take our places as prophetic intercessors *and* interceptors. I want to intercept the plans of the enemy and intercede for the fulfillment of God's purposes. What is His ultimate aim? *"But truly, as I live, all the earth shall be filled with the glory of the Lord"* (Num. 14:21 NKJV). We don't stop praying and obeying until we see Heaven have measurable impact and influence on every arena of society.

The prophets have taken their place by submitting these words. Now I encourage you, as believers in Jesus and as prophetic people, receive these words with prayerful discernment. Pray through them. Ask the Holy Spirit how you can embrace the invitations being extended through each unique prophetic voice. Here's the deal: the high benchmark of the prophetic movement is *not* how spiritual our words sound or how supernatural our experiences with God are. Rather, the benchmark of the prophetic should be *how does society look and function more like Heaven because prophets are receiving and releasing intel from God that, when prayed and practiced, releases measurable Kingdom transformation.*

I believe it was Cindy Jacobs who commented that the prophet's report card is the newspaper. In other words, what we see happening or not happening in the world can be influenced by a prophetic voice that prays, speaks, and partners with the Word of the Lord. My prayer for you is that you would receive these prophetic words, embrace them (as you are directed and led by the Holy Spirit), and take ownership of the different Kingdom realities they present. It's not enough just to read them and be encouraged; may we be motivated to respond and participate!

Chapter 1

FIVE WAYS THE DEVIL IS TRYING TO TURN CHRISTIANITY UPSIDE DOWN

Larry Sparks

Sid Roth looked at me and asked, "Larry, what is the Lord saying to you right now?" I did not expect *this* to come out of my mouth.

When bringing a "hard" prophetic word, I believe there needs to be a few elements involved in the presentation. Of course, the content needs to be accurate. Second, the content must be paired with the "tone" of the Lord. God's heart breaks over these things, as should ours, as the Lord does not want *"any to perish but all to come to repentance"* (2 Pet. 3:9 CSB).

With every warning, confrontation, and challenge should come a *redemptive solution*. It doesn't take a prophet to call out the obvious problems in the world or church; it does demand true prophetic acumen, however, to hear Heaven's solutions on how to reverse the problem, be it anything from personal sin, church compromise, or some kind of impending global catastrophe.

PROPHETS: FRIENDS WHO RECEIVE SECRETS

Prophecy, in short, is never delivered for the purpose of being able to deliver a spiritual "I told you so" when a negative reality ultimately comes to pass. That's not the sign of an accurate prophet. Sure, the event or item foretold came to pass, but God raises up prophets to do at least two things: see what the enemy has coming and prevent it, and see what God desires to release into the Earth and partner with it. One way or another, as a prophet you will see or hear things in the spirit. You will hear of things to come. This is a fundamental, non-negotiable element of prophetic ministry. It's not being some prognosticator or predictor; it's being one who is sensitive to the voice of the Holy Spirit, who Jesus said would lead us into all truth and *"he will tell you what is yet to come"* (John 16:13 NIV) or *"He will tell you about the future"* (NLT).

When the Lord gives us insight into what is coming, our first response should *not* be to share it in the public forum and call it a prophecy. We only share what we believe the Spirit of God has told us to share, and before doing so, I strongly recommend that prophets submit their words to other reputable and respected prophets. The goal of prophecy is not immediately sharing it; it's translating what Heaven is entrusting to you. It's a summons to dialogue with the Holy Spirit. We need to wrestle with Heaven for clarity on the purpose or assignment of a prophetic word. We're so quick to want to push the "share" button on whatever we receive because we live in a day and age when people become overnight sensations because of their spectacular revelatory and prophetic insights. Before one is a prophet, he or she is first a *friend of God* like Moses and Abraham. Friends share secrets with their friends—why? Because friends can be trusted with such precious intel. Likewise, the Lord shares His secrets with His friends, those who fear Him, because He is looking for one in the Earth to trust with what He is saying and doing.

Consider the dynamics of Psalm 25:14 from three translations of the passage.

> *The secret of the Lord is with them that fear him; and he will shew them his covenant* (Psalm 25:14 KJV).

First, we read about an exchange between the Lord and those He considers to be friends. This is a place of deep intimacy between God and man. Who are granted access to "the secret of the Lord"? Those who *fear Him.*

> *The Lord is a friend to those who fear him* (Psalm 25:14 NLT).

Second, we discover that those who fear the Lord are the friends of God. This almost sounds paradoxical. How can we be friends with someone we're afraid of? A biblical definition of the fear of the Lord or holy fear is *not* being scared of God, thus causing us to draw back; it's about honoring and revering the Lord and thus drawing near acceptably. We draw near to One who is King and God. He deserves to be revered as such. The blood of Jesus has granted us access into the Presence of the Lord, absolutely. But what posture will we assume as we enter into this sacred dimension of access? Leviticus 10:3 is an Old Covenant principle that is still applicable to the New Covenant priesthood. We are all priests before the Lord because of Jesus' atoning work. However, there is a protocol to approaching the King of Glory: *"This is what the Lord said: 'I will be treated as holy by those who approach Me'"* (Lev. 10:3 AMP).

Consider how *The Passion Translation* presents Psalm 25:14: *"There's a private place reserved for the lovers of God, where they sit near him and receive the revelation-secrets of his promises."* Prophets are intimate friends of God. Their hearts are anchored in the fear of the Lord; thus, they approach God as One who is holy. This posture, not their self-proclaimed title as "prophet," is what qualifies them to receive secrets from Heaven. And such secrets are entrusted to those who will not become spiritual blabbermouths the first chance they get. When God entrusts us with secrets that involve confrontation, warning, or words that are more of a hard nature, our first response should never be to shout it from the mountaintop. Rather, we need to process it with God, ask the Holy Spirit for translation, and then, perhaps more importantly, seek the Lord for redemptive solutions to accompany the confrontational word.

DEBATE OR DISTRACTION?

I'll be honest—this particular word came to me in the midst of frustration.

I have noticed, more and more, that particular movements in the body of Christ that place a biblical emphasis on gifts of the Spirit (continuationism) along with experiencing "manifestations of the Spirit" (physical evidences of people being touched the Holy Spirit's power) are under fresh attack by both "heresy hunters" and some reputable evangelical leaders. This is unfortunate. Not because we shouldn't discuss or debate these items. I think we absolutely should. And not in the shadows, but in the public square. But we should discuss and passionately debate these topics *as family*, not foes intent on destroying or demonizing one another. The family conversation is not taking place. In fact, we're not seeing intelligent discussion or well-researched debate going on; we are witnessing hate speech turned demonization, which is really poor taste for any self-proclaimed Christian to resort to when it comes to lambasting fellow believers engaging in charismatic practices. We need to stop this adolescence immediately, as it wars against the fulfillment of the high priestly prayer of Messiah Jesus: *"that they may be one, even as we are one"* (John 17:11).

What's the big deal? Our inability to discuss and debate as brothers and sisters in Christ has ultimately played into satan's objective for America (and, ultimately, other nations). While we are engaged in petty arguments over differences in the non-essentials of the faith, I believe there are at least five insidious weapons the devil is aiming at modern Christianity. He'd love to keep us distracted, squabbling amongst ourselves while he literally reinvents and reconstructs the Christian faith and thus renders the church ineffective to help bring about Kingdom transformation in every cultural sphere.

While we devote endless hours to propagating articles, blogs, videos, audios, interviews, and yes entire websites and "discernment ministries," the devil is quickly becoming the architect behind the cultures, moral values, and belief systems of nations. Nations are being discipled, yes—just *not* by those who were anointed and commissioned to disciple the nations. While we (yes, Christians) are busy demonizing one another, actual demons are out controlling the societal airways. This has got to stop!

As of 2020, this list consists of *five ways the devil is trying to turn Christianity upside down* and thus short-circuit the Kingdom impact that we are very capable of having in the world. Sadly, I can see this list growing if we don't rise up as a unified church and collaboratively take the fight to the gates of hell. This is when warfare becomes offensive; now, it's often defensive. Much of our spiritual warfare (albeit necessary) is cleaning up messes made by the devil in our lives and in our nations. I'm not content with this. Jesus gave us a warfare paradigm that we are living beneath. In modern terms, He said "take the fight to the enemy's gates." This demands a unified people, however. The devil is defeated, yes, but he is powerful. He is a formidable foe. Yet the church has what it takes to dispose of his influence.

Five Ways the Devil Is Trying to Turn Christianity Upside Down

1. Universalism

This is the belief that everyone gets into Heaven regardless of their response to the Gospel. There are multiple dimensions to this destructive heresy. Some claim that the atonement is all-encompassing; thus, every human being throughout history experiences immediate salvation because of Jesus' work. Yes, His atoning work on the cross was more than sufficient to cover all the sins of all of humanity throughout all of time. However, in order to *receive* this glorious gift, we need to place *saving faith* in Jesus. I can side with both my Reformed and Arminian friends here. Whether God gave you the ability to place faith in the Gospel or you exercised some kind of free will, either way the Gospel demands a choice, and that choice should be evidenced by a transformed life.

2. The "deconstruction of the Christian faith"

This "deconstruction" terminology is relatively new language, but I am seeing it more and more prevalent among young people. There are two dimensions here. For one, there is a healthy form of deconstruction, where we take inventory of what we believe, measure our beliefs and theology beside the Bible, and make sure what we believe lines up with what is written in Scripture. We are conforming our beliefs to the Bible. Ultimately, religion is not our foundation. Tradition is not our cornerstone. The way we've always done things does not have the final say, *unless* our religion, tradition, and methodologies are in pure agreement with the Word of God.

The second dimension, however, is where the devil is using this deconstruction/reconstruction language to his advantage right now. In this age of increasing compromise, I am seeing more and more self-proclaimed Christians actually deny or reject certain cardinal tenants of the Christian faith, not because they have disproved them from the Bible. The opposite. Truths like eternal judgment, hell, sin, gender, sexual standards, and other realities are not considered politically correct today. They are not comfortable; thus, because they do not align with where culture is going, we decide that Scripture has become irrelevant to speak to these certain matters. As a result, we "deconstruct our faith," adjusting the Bible to accommodate our preferences. Result? We end up with a Christian faith that is a destructive composite of biblical truth and demonic error. Perhaps the great sin of deconstruction is dethroning the lordship of Jesus and thus falling into idolatry. No, we are not worshiping statues or graven images, but we have replaced the authority of King Jesus with the authority of our feelings, our preferences, and what the world says is acceptable.

3. An imbalanced Gospel

I want to tread very carefully here. In Romans 12:1, Paul tells us that in view or consideration of God's mercy, we should offer up our lives as living sacrifices. A weightless, ambiguous, flighty "Gospel" message does not provoke us to offer up our lives; if anything, such a message can easily breed complacency and compromise. At its core, the Gospel is the message of salvation from the condemnation that our sin deserves.

Ephesians 2 provides some of the most compelling and striking language of what's at the heart of this glorious Gospel. We were dead in our sins and trespasses (see Eph. 2:1), hopelessly cut off from the life of God (see Eph. 2:12). We were doomed and damned, not because of an unloving God but because our hearts were infected by sin and deserved righteous judgment from the Just Judge. While we were yet sinners, God still loved us and Christ died for us! (See Romans 5:8.) However, we were dead in our sins, and if that's true, well—dead people don't have much decision-making capability. We don't wake up one day and have some bright idea to simply "go with God." Salvation is a profoundly supernatural work wrought by the regenerating power of the Holy Spirit.

This is the Gospel. Yes, our response to the Gospel produces many amazing blessings such as freedom, deliverance, healing, abundant life, joy, fulfillment, satisfaction, God's Presence in our lives, etc. But at its core, the Gospel is *not* "I've been saved from a mediocre life and now, because of Jesus, I get to live happy and satisfied." This is imbalance. Jesus didn't die for me simply to live a happy or "full" life; He died so that a spiritually doomed, hell-bound sinner could be redeemed from the eternal punishment that sin deserves. He shed His precious blood so that a new temple could be established, not one built by the hands of men but one fashioned by the hands of the Creator—you and I. He purified this temple with His blood and thus made our physical bodies a compatible resting place for the Holy Spirit's indwelling Presence. Why is our vision of the Gospel so important? Simple. Our vision of the Gospel will always determine the lifestyle of faith we manifest. If our Gospel is weak, flimsy, and all about *me*, then our Christian walk will be likewise.

4. *Redefinition of sin*

We are no longer calling sin what it is—*sin*. This is exactly what satan wants. We don't preach sin to make people feel bad; we preach sin to make people recognize their state of absolute spiritual bankruptcy and desperation, for which Jesus' blood is the only remedy. Sin is *not* an "oops" or a "fail" or a "boo boo." We cannot trivialize sin. All sin is damning and destructive. What happens when we start redefining sin, calling that which is destructive progressive, tolerant, acceptable, and culturally relevant? We begin redefining sin to meet our current cultural preferences. Whether it's the redefinition of marriage, gender, or even life, we have no right to move the ancient boundary lines—those standards and definitions that the Creator established as life-giving and life-enhancing. To believe we have any right or ability to redefine sin is to play God, and once again we become guilty of blatant idolatry.

I can give you one very clear reason why the devil wants us to redefine sin and completely remove the language of "repentance" from the Christian faith. If we start erasing Bible standards and rather adjust the Bible to agree with cultural preferences or even how we feel about something, then we begin calling evil good. We start calling sin acceptable. This is heinous for believers because sin is what gives satan legal right into our lives, and unless we repent he will enter in without opposition and claim as much territory as possible, ultimately culminating with personal destruction and creating inroads for future generations to suffer the same bondage. The sin issue is *not* a love issue. Your sin does not impact God's love toward you one iota. However, living in sin does prevent us from experiencing and enjoying the love of God, and also, it continues to grant darkness legal permission to wreak havoc in our lives.

5. *A disconnected and disengaged church*

The present state of society should tell us that something is wrong when it comes to the church's impact on the world. We *need* the church, now more than ever. Buildings are fine! Programs are great! Delivering excellent production value is totally acceptable! But let's be totally honest—four songs, entertaining production value, twenty bucks in an offering bucket, and inspiring life lessons *alone* will not shift society. We have church buildings on every street corner, but how many cities have actually experienced true revival, awakening, and even reformation—at least in modern times?

Here's the deal: I know we like to evaluate the impact of our church services and gatherings based on how well the "weekend worship experience" went. Yes, we need to evaluate these elements for administrative purposes and to maintain environments of excellence, but they are *not* the definitive measuring standards for the effectiveness of the church. It's time for a new metric of evaluation— the condition of our society, Monday through Saturday, reveals the level of impact our churches are having. What do our cities look like? How about the schools and education system? What's the crime rate like? From serving the homeless with the compassion of Jesus to offering prophetically inspired business strategies in high-rise boardrooms, the church, the ecclesia, must be making a measurable imprint upon society; otherwise, we drift into irrelevance (regardless of how relevant we claim to be in our spiritual presentation). Simply put, the church needs to arise and define itself by Jesus' standard in

Matthew 16—an *ecclesia*. Ed Silvoso describes this as a mobile people movement that has impact on everyone, *everywhere.* Yes!

When I was confronted with these five things, I felt overwhelmed. But when the Lord delivers a prophetic warning or confrontation, He never leaves us without hope. I believe an essential element of the prophetic is being able to access solutions and strategies from Heaven that reverse the present conditions. So, what's the solution?

The solution is *not* prayer alone, although prayer and intercession are vital.

The solution is *not* more supernatural meetings, miracle conferences, or prophetic events, although they are vital points of convergence to unite, train, and deploy the people.

The solution is *not* simply laying back and accepting the horrors plaguing society as merely "signs of the end

> The solution is, and has always been, an engaged, unified remnant.

times," although we are obviously living in the "last days" as defined by the Bible (the period of time between Pentecost and the return of Jesus).

When Jesus describes His people or the entity of the church, He uses language that describes a transformational community.

In Matthew 5:13-16, Jesus describes His people as the *salt of the Earth* and *light of the world.* Note the words "earth" and "world." The presence of a Holy Spirit-filled, Jesus-commissioned people on planet Earth should have a measurable impact. The world should be brighter and the Earth should have a lot more flavor because the Spirit of God is actively at work in society through a mobile temple called born-again believers.

The solution is the ecclesia, the church Jesus defined in Matthew 16, unifying around the core non-negotiables of the faith, advancing together to see every soul redeemed and every cultural system impacted by the Gospel of the Kingdom.

The Lord gave me this encouragement following the formation of the confrontational prophetic word you just reviewed: "The solution to crisis has always been a remnant. And the remnant is bigger than you think!" It's not a couple of lone ranger Christians here and there, hunkered down just trying to make do until Jesus comes back. The devil is aiming at the unification of God's remnant, doing whatever he can to bring disunity the body of Christ—using the five strategies listed above. Why? Because when we operate and function *as one*, the prayer of Jesus is fulfilled, glory is manifested to the Earth, and no soul or nation is safe from the transformational power of King Jesus.

> *I do not ask for these only, but also for those who will believe in me through their word, that they may all be one, just as you, Father, are in me, and I in you, that they also may be in us, so that the world may believe that you have sent me. The glory that you have given me I have given to them, that they may be one even as we are one* (John 17:20-22).

> *Lord, raise up a unified remnant so that the body of Christ boldly arises, preaches truth without compromise, operates in the supernatural power of God, and once again becomes a life-preserving force to society!*

Chapter 2

The Beginning of the Days of Holy Power

Emma Stark

Recently I heard the terrifyingly awesome sound of an enormous bomb going off in the spirit realm. As the bomb exploded, its effects ricocheted around the whole globe. And the Spirit of the Lord said to me, "This bomb marks the beginning of the *days of holy power* in the earth, and I am now branding a generation of leaders who will carry a new anointing of holy power."

God said, "I will burn their flesh. They will not become puffed-up individuals who only get more independent over time. Instead, My anointing on them will be like an acid poured over them until any partnership with the enemy and with past pain is dissolved.

In turn, they will lead a new breed of church, where My holy power does not just have signs, wonders, and miracles accompanying it, as you were expecting, but will be churches who also know the dissolving of sin and of pride and that which does not fully give all of its attention and glory to God."

If you have recently entered a season of personal soul-searching or have been feeling overwhelmed; if you have been aware of an intensity that exposes; if you have had to face your issues in a new way—well done! You are right on time with God as He marks us to carry holy power.

He is squeezing you through a narrow place now so that you will carry His undiluted nature. God is "pressing all of our buttons" and is even allowing us to become frustrated. By doing so, He is helping us to acknowledge the limitations of the current place that we are in. It is a time of *straining and stretching,* and for many it will feel like we have been thrown up in the air and are wondering where we will land!

THE POST-PENTECOSTAL, POST-CHARISMATIC CHURCH

God has not let some things work out up to this point because this year we will go *beyond* "Pentecostal" and *beyond* "Charismatic" frameworks. We are birthing a post-Pentecostal, post-Charismatic church, and many will want to change their church names, as a result, in order to better represent this era. A whole new breed of church—and new networks of church—will arise, whose focus will be *holy power*—displaying the abilities of God.

This is not just re-brand but re-birth.

Force Will Stop the Enemy

Our enemy, satan, has no language for surrender. He does not know how to stop or submit; he does not know how to capitulate or concede. We never read anything in the Word of God about an enemy who backs down willingly. In fact, we read of the enemy referred to as *on the prowl* (see 1 Pet. 5:8) and acting fast with great fury, knowing that his time is short (see Rev. 12:2).

Similarly, throughout history Japanese warriors, from the samurai to the kamikaze pilots, have had no language of surrender, even in the face of defeat. It is in their DNA to never, ever back down or concede defeat. This sounds like an impressive mindset; however, it caused President Truman of the United States a great dilemma in the final months of World War II.

The war in Europe ceased when Germany signed its "instrument of surrender" on May 8, 1945. But an agreement like this would never work with the Japanese who, two months later, would still not contemplate surrender.

How does one make a people yield who don't know how? How do you make satan yield when it is not his way?

In summer 1945, Truman made the decision of his life. It must have been a horrifically difficult, agonizing choice, but in the end he choose to display such an awesome force of power that his enemy would have no option but to lay down their arms.

As we know, on August 6 and 9, the US detonated two nuclear weapons over the Japanese cities of Hiroshima and Nagasaki. Truman and his military had introduced a level of power that forced their enemy to back down.

This year, we, the church, will introduce a level of power that is so vastly superior in force that the enemy will back down. It is why we are told to "wrestle" in Ephesians:

> *For we do not wrestle against flesh and blood, but against principalities, against powers, against the rulers of the darkness of this age, against spiritual hosts of wickedness in the heavenly places* (Ephesians 6:12 NKJV).

Nowadays we think of "wrestle" as suggesting a fight of some equality, but to Paul it actually meant "to hold the enemy down with your hand upon his neck." In other words, to force a surrender with your display of power.

Through us, His church, God will cause public displays of power in order to teach an un-retreating enemy exactly who the Boss is. It will be a shocking power.

This is not physical violence or bloody warfare (*our struggle is not against flesh and blood*). Instead, we will drop bombs of prayer, drop bombs of prophecy, drop bombs of miracles, and drop bombs of deliverance.

A People of Power and Purity

God is helping us to shift our mindset into becoming and being *people of power*. This is a mindset of knowing that you carry the power and favor of God that can bring *real change*. It is an anointing of *force* to achieve what needs to be done. But it is also an inner knowing that "*this thing I'm tasked with will be accomplished.*" It is a stance of certainty that will see new victories for the people of God.

> *Your people will volunteer freely in the day of Your power* (Psalm 110:3 NASB).

The church will spontaneously and freely—willingly—opt in as the might, strength, and power of God are displayed!

How do you get the church behaving as she should? You display the power of God and the church will come out of hiding!

We are moving from individual stories where a life got changed here, a life got changed there into stories of changed *regions* and changed *nations* as we show what our Father can do.

A Pivot Year

We are entering one of the most strategic years of our entire lives. We will need *sobriety*, *focus,* and *alertness*—as this year will shape us for many years to come. This year will be recorded in history as a *pivot year.*

God is talking us into something outrageous this year and many will step into roles that they aren't yet comfortable with. *You* will be stepping into new places that are not your norm. *You* are stepping into a season that you are not comfortable with. You will feel gloriously uncomfortable! But this "uncomfortableness" is a gift that will keep you moving.

The verse that God has given me for the year is:

> *Our God comes and will not be silent; a fire devours before him, and around him a tempest rages* (Psalm 50:3 NIV).

The booming voice of God will be heard. He will come close, scorching and devouring. *Purity* will be established, and storms of change will be the norm. "New" really will mean "new"!

Waging War on the Evolutionary Spirit

I heard God say, "The church has partnered with an evolutionary spirit."

This is not that the church is believing in evolution, but rather that it has been partnering with the demonic spirit behind evolutionary theory. This spirit shapes us to believe in "the survival of the fittest" so we don't behave in an interconnected, dependent-on-each-other way. This one spirit has shut down our aliveness to the supernatural realm (and therefore the miraculous) because it gives us a value for our own strength.

It is happy when we sit filling our minds with information, which has become the goal of many of our church gatherings. God is waging war on this with us and for us. The church will come into a time of repentance this year for limiting the supernatural and those who value it. There will be public apologies from leaders as this spirit breaks, and a new openness to the spiritual dimension amongst the wider family of the people of God will arise!

On the other hand, God is asking the Spirit-filled church to *grow up*. Rather than a fixation on the spectacular, she will gain an ease with the supernatural and attain a new level of maturity in these things.

THE SECOND WAVE OF THE PROPHETIC MOVEMENT

We are in the second wave of the prophetic movement. We are *growing up* to understanding that prophets will speak and steward the destiny of nations—and they will not just *build up*, but they will also *tear down* (see Jer. 1:10). This year revelation will partner with power, just as Moses modelled.

> *Believe His prophets, and you shall prosper* (2 Chronicles 20:20 NKJV).

You need to pay attention to this verse because God is giving extreme words to His prophetic people in extreme times. It is only in the day of the *outlandish* prophecies and impossible words that we need a verse like this.

Therefore, expect ridiculous words—extreme words—to come from out of your mouth! Expect God to test your obedience in delivering these words. He's going to ask you in increasingly yielded increments. When He asks, "Will you say this *hard* thing?" or, "Will you say this *impossible* thing?"—how will you answer?

DANIEL AND THE WEIGHTY WORDS

I was caught up to heaven during a time of worship. God allowed me to observe the prophet Daniel, who was looking at all the revelation that God wanted released in the coming year. And the Lord said, "I have tasked Daniel to decide who gets each piece of this revelation because he knows what it is to walk the earth with the weight of extreme revelation." Daniel was weeping as he assigned each revelation to those on the earth, knowing that it would *cost* those who held it and spoke it out. God said, "Get the people to ask for strength to carry weighty words this year."

TRUTH WILL NOT BE AN OFFENSE

In the UK, where I live, we are now called a "pre-Christian" society. This generation in the world is largely in ignorance and delusion about the body of Christ. However, the world will see this year that His people are good and that there is something sweet and victorious that they carry.

People will ask to hear us *speak truth*. Truth will not be an offense to the world. Instead, truth will be seen as redemptive and necessary; truth will be pleasing and urgently desired.

You have a sound that God is getting ready to present to the earth. You are going to be presented to the world as a voice!

THE SECOND WAVE OF THE DELIVERANCE MOVEMENT

We are in the second wave of the deliverance movement. No longer will we spend hours getting one person free. We are *growing up* and this year we will receive an anointing for the mass deliverance of people and also to set land and nations free!

I saw the "angel of awakening" and the "angel of harvest" that have already been sent to the earth and they were joined by the "angel of deliverance"—a triune angelic strike force for this year! The "angel of deliverance" was accompanied by a battalion of destroyer angels—the category of angel that destroyed Sodom and Gomorrah. And the angel said, "My job is to destroy the works of the accuser of the brethren. Call the church army to partner with me. God has tasked me with releasing a deliverance mindset to His people."

> *The Son of Man will send out his angels, and they will weed out of his kingdom everything that causes sin and all who do evil* (Matthew 13:41 NIV).

We will receive an ability to think as deliverers this year who instinctively set captives free. Churches who have not been familiar with deliverance will be moved by God toward it.

We will see this deliverance anointing come to our worship and captives will be set free in the middle of church services. Demons will flee because of the anointing that will be released!

Expect to feel "shot" during worship as the angels fire at the demons in you. Expect to fall on the floor as the angels kick the demons out of your life! There will be a descending of the *Lord Sabaoth*, the Lord of War, and of the angel armies as we worship.

THE SECOND WAVE OF THE APOSTOLIC

We are in the second wave of the apostolic, shifting on from finding, naming, and raising apostles. Now the apostolic will *grow up* and people will start being sent!

Heaven looked busier than usual recently and God was standing over a map of the earth. His glory touched it and He released a *sending anointing* that got behind people and surged them into a new location. We are going to see the mass movement of people into new nations, new jobs, and new locations for the sake of the gospel of the Kingdom.

God is calling many to be citizens of more than one nation, simultaneously. There is a blessing on travel visas for those God moves.

The *suddenly* of God will shift many in short time frames. In four to six months, many will move house and new buildings for ministries and churches will quickly come into our hands. This is a *geographical relocation* time. God asks us, *"Do you want to be with Me where I am? Will you follow, even though it looks foggy and the end point is not clear?"*

THE SECOND WAVE OF THE
INTERCESSORY MOVEMENT

We are in the second wave of the intercessory movement. I heard trumpets blast around the throne of God, the sound that begins new eras. Seven trumpeters who initiated a new anointing for the watchmen prophetic intercessors. Each of the seven trumpets also represented an earthquake that God had sent during biblical times.

Watchmen prophetic intercessors, you are now going to initiate earthquakes in the spiritual realm that will be cataclysmic for the enemy. Your traps and your sieges will shake his very foundations!

The anointing to make the earthquake is upon you, watchmen! The anointing to shake foundations is yours! You will know *offensive dominance*—where you will kill the enemy in the shortest period of time.

CHILDREN, PARENTS, AND GRANDPARENTS

I saw God group His people together, according to their age. He gave a special grace to each age group. The 20- to 40-year-old group He called "children"—and they received a grace for *holy experimenting.* They will come back to a slow, steady burn of the Word of the Lord rather than a fast-paced, "microwave" lifestyle. There will be a replacement of social media with the Word of God.

The 40- to 60-year-olds He called "parents." Many of this group have been forgotten, overlooked, and are waiting, because many of them have never fully come into their place.

They will receive a grace to *build*. God shouted, *"Build, build, build!"* over them. Stop waiting for the permission of men when the permission of God has already been granted! Stop looking and start building! Revelation will become an activation.

Those aged 60 year and over He called "grandparents" and they received a new grace to *advise* without undermining the new. And with ease they were being moved by God to let go of what they had pioneered and stewarded so well and had held on to for too long.

God expects different things from each age group. He was reordering His people to flow and to support each other and not to undermine each other's development.

Let God shift you into the extreme of 2020 as you live through the pivot year.

ABOUT EMMA STARK

Emma Stark is a prophet who operates with authority and authenticity as she ministers and teaches around the world. Born in Northern Ireland into a long family line of church pastors, Emma communicates with clarity, humour and Celtic boldness!

She and her husband are founding directors of *Glasgow Prophetic Centre*. Thousands from around the world have travelled to their centre in Scotland to hear from God, receive freedom and be trained and activated in prophecy, revelation and spiritual warfare.

Chapter 3

PROPHETIC ACCURACY, JEALOUSY, AND POLITICAL TURMOIL

Jeremiah Johnson

PROPHETIC ACCURACY

As I prayed into 2020, I was immediately directed to 1 Corinthians 14:25, which says that the secrets of their hearts were exposed and they will fall down to worship God exclaiming, "God is really among us." Throughout 2020, there will be a realm of prophetic accuracy that the Body of Christ has not felt in recent years. Large portions of the Charismatic church have become so accustomed to vague, fortune-cookie, and generalized prophecy that rarely comes to pass that when accurate and specific prophecy comes forth, they reject it on the basis of "needing to test all things" when the only thing that needs testing is their own heart who now despises prophecy.

It's so true! There are thousands of saints who have followed prophets for many years in the past who were just plain *off*. Their "prophecies" could be applied to just about anything and then when they tried to get specific they totally missed it.

I've got news for the Charismatic church—we are entering into a new era prophetically in 2020 where true and authentic prophets of God are going to rise who will hit the *bull's-eye* again and again. They will prophesy accurately and specifically concerning politics, media, and the future of the Church. It's called revelatory prophecy. Not the spontaneous kind that most are used to that is borderline psychic palm reading.

Many that once followed prophets and even those who flowed in prophecy years ago will accuse these emerging prophets of being "arrogant" when really these voices are simply confident that they actually hear the voice of God and they don't need to prophesy for money or fame. If God said it, that settles it. Authentic prophets do not take polls or waste time arguing with internet trolls. It's going to be incredible to watch what God does with prophetic accuracy in 2020.

A SPIRIT OF JEALOUSY

The next thing that God brought before me as I sought Him concerning what was going to be happening in the Body of Christ in 2020 was a major spirit of jealously being stirred up among leaders and people.

James 3:14-16 says, *"But if you harbor bitter envy and selfish ambition in your hearts, do not boast about it or deny the truth. Such 'wisdom' does not come down from heaven but is earthly, unspiritual, demonic. For where you have envy and selfish ambition, there you find disorder and every evil practice"* (NLT).

Jealousy is a very powerful and deceptive sin. It will cause you to believe that everyone who has more success and influence than you do is filled with pride and arrogance. The truth is that their outward promotion is just revealing our inward commotion.

Remember, insecure people always interpret the victories of others as an indictment on their failures. Their defense mechanism will be to attack and criticize the very people who are modeling for them where God is calling them. It's sick and twisted. Hiding deep behind the accusation of a jealous heart toward someone is really anger and resentment that they aren't them. We want their influence. We want their success. And we will deny it vehemently.

Jealousy oftentimes manifests as fear or resentment of another's success, speaking against the person, going on a vendetta to hurt their credibility, keeping them from being admired, or actually engaging in a conspiracy to kill their public image. Jealousy oftentimes diverts us from receiving solid truth merely because we have an issue with the person who states it.

Political Turmoil

In my new book, *Trump and the Future of America*, I share a detailed series of revelatory dreams and visions concerning the political climate in the US as well as what God is saying to the Church in this hour.

Going into the 2020 election, there will be great turmoil and upheaval in the news concerning the Presidency. In a recent dream, I saw Donald Trump running in a huge marathon. He was being spit on by the crowds on all sides as he ran down the finish line. About 100 feet from the finish, he collapsed and everyone started to cheer. Two old women with visible limitations because of their age somehow got Donald Trump up on his feet and dragged him across the finish line just in time.

Waking up from the dream, I felt an intense burden that if the intercessors (the two old women) do not rise and come to the aid of Donald Trump, he will be in serious trouble in 2020 concerning the elections. While the crowds will jeer and shout at him, he is in desperate need of the Church to assist him in finishing the race God has set before him.

Look for prophetic accuracy and the timing of prophetic fulfillment to greatly increase in 2020. What will be prophesied will take mere days and weeks to be fulfilled in the news and in people's lives. We must also be on guard against jealously. It will manifest both personally and in attacks against us. We must be reminded that it is demonic and needs to be exposed in our lives. It is the hidden sin that many do not want to talk about. Finally, let us keep President Donald Trump in great prayer and fasting in 2020. The political turmoil will only increase in the US and the intercessors must assist him in completing the assignment God has given him for the nation.

ABOUT JEREMIAH JOHNSON

Jeremiah Johnson planted and is the overseer of Heart of the Father Ministry in Lakeland, Florida. A gifted teacher, prophet, and author of multiple books, Jeremiah travels extensively throughout the United States and abroad as a conference and guest speaker. He has been a guest on Christian television and radio shows including *The Jim Bakker Show*, Sid Roth's *It's Supernatural!*, and *The Line of Fire* with Dr. Michael Brown, as well as on networks such as Daystar, TBN, and God TV. Jeremiah is also the founder and director of Maranatha School of Ministry. MSM is a full-time, five-fold ministry training center that equips and sends out end-time messengers. For more information, please visit jeremiahjohnson.tv or www. maranatha.school. Jeremiah and his wife, Morgan, reside in Florida with their four children.

Chapter 4

2020: The Year of Bold Faith

Lana Vawser

The Lord spoke to me recently that 2020 will be a year of *bold faith*.

In 2020 and beyond the body of Christ is going to be brought into a season of understanding in greater ways the truth of 2 Corinthians 5:7:

> *For we walk by faith, not by sight* (NASB).

> *For we live by faith, not by what we see with our eyes* (TPT).

In this new era that we have entered into there have been many battles that many have been facing in the body of Christ, and amidst all the trials, battles, oppositions and tribulations the Lord has been doing a deep work within the hearts of His people, inviting them into a realm of faith that they have not walked in before. The Holy Spirit whispered to me halfway through 2019: "Lana, I am bringing My people into a place called *resistance training*." The heart of the Lord in that word was that He is building a people who live so deeply rooted and anchored in faith that with every trial, battle, and opposition they face their "faith muscles" get stronger and stronger because they are living not by what they *see* in the natural, but by what they *see* in the Spirit. In all things that the enemy meant for harm, the Lord is truly turning for good (see Gen. 50:20) and drawing His people into a place of fortified faith unlike anything they have ever walked in before.

The Spirit of God is working deeply in the hearts of His people in this new era that we have entered into, stirring a "no tolerance" for anything that opposes the promises of God. He is developing within His people a roar that says "*No!* I will not tolerate or accept this because it is contrary to what the Lord has spoken and is speaking."

> Our authority level in Christ is connected to our level of faith. To the degree we believe God's word, we will obey and act upon it with authority. Grow in your faith and thereby, grow in your authority in Christ.
> —DUTCH SHEETS, *Authority in Prayer*

In many ways, 2020 is going to be a year of significant alignment. It is going to be a year of key alignments where the Lord is going to position His people in greater ways to walk in greater manifestation of their destiny and His plans and purposes. The level of acceleration and move of the Spirit of God in the lives of His people, in the Church, and in the earth will be unlike anything we have ever seen before. We have entered a completely new era and it requires a deeper place of having our ear upon His chest to hear what He is saying and walking by faith in every word that flows from His mouth (see Matt. 4:4).

The Lord showed me that this deep fortification and maturing of faith taking place in the lives of believers must take place for us to be positioned and ready to partner with Him in what will be the greatest move of the Spirit of God in the earth, unlike anything that we have ever seen.

2020 will be a year to not only take back what has been stolen but to occupy new territories and new lands. The Lord has been thundering the word *established* to me regarding many things for the body of Christ. In 2020 there will be an *establishing* into the territories, new lands, and promises God has for His people without being "uprooted."

> *"I will plant them on their land, and they shall never again be uprooted out of the land that I have given them," says the Lord your God* (Amos 9:15).

There is an establishing and an occupying that is going to take place in 2020 and beyond for the people of God walking in a greater measure of their authority, identity, and destiny.

THE POWER OF THE MUSTARD SEED

I heard the Holy Spirit say, "In 2020 I will demonstrate the power of the mustard seed."

For truly, I say to you, if you have faith like a grain of mustard seed, you will say to this mountain, "Move from here to there," and it will move, and nothing will be impossible for you (Matthew 17:20).

I promise you, if you have faith inside of you no bigger than the size of a small mustard seed, you can say to this mountain, "Move away from here and go over there," and you will see it move. There is nothing you couldn't do! (Matthew 17:20 TPT)

The Lord will do an even deeper work in maturing the saints in faith in 2020 that will be one of the ways the Lord *reintroduces the Church to His power.* For what is ahead and the glory of God being manifested and unveiled across the earth and the nations that we are going to see in this new era, the Church must be a people who are engaging with the heart of God and living by the *rhema* word of God and are not shaken by circumstances. The Lord is doing a solidifying work within His people now to prepare us to partner with Him in seeing explosive demonstrations of His power across the earth. The Lord is not looking for a weak bride who is tired, weary, and disappointed. He is breaking off all the hope deferred and things that have hindered and lingered. He is preparing and raising up a Church who takes the Lord at His Word and moves on it with a fire of conviction that makes them unshakeable and unmovable and partners with Him to see impossibilities bow to the name of Jesus.

In the demonstration of the power of the mustard seed, the Lord will not only reintroduce the Church to His power but also to the *power of the Word of God.* In 2020 and beyond the Lord is going to reintroduce the people of God to the power of the Word of God. There will be a significant impartation of faith and conviction from the Holy Spirit in 2020 in lives of believers to *see* that the Word *works!* (See Hebrews 4:12.) Disappointment and hope deferred will no longer be part of the story but a fire of conviction and passion in the power of the Word of God to see impossibilities bow.

"KNOW MY WAYS"

The Lord continues to speak to me for 2020 and this new era about the invitation to "know His ways" like never before. This invitation being extended to us in 2020 and beyond is to be schooled by the Holy Spirit in the ways of God. To engage with His heart and His wisdom in a way we never have before.

> *"For My thoughts are not your thoughts, nor are your ways My ways" declares the Lord* (Isaiah 55:8 NASB).

It is imperative in 2020 and beyond that we have our ears to His chest and are living in the truth that we have been given the mind of Christ (see 1 Cor. 2:16) and are seeking the wisdom of God (see James 1:5). There is a yielding to the ways of God that will be required from God's people in 2020 and beyond. It is a place where God will have you step out of the boat. It will be a place of stepping into new ways of building with Him. It will be a place of stepping into new assignments and things

> Some of the greatest demonstrations of His power and the power of His Word bringing impossibilities down will be seen in 2020 and beyond.

you never imagined. It will be a place of having to trust the wisdom of God and the ways of God rather than any "wisdom of man." There will be many blueprints the Lord will download in 2020 and beyond that will require you and I to "go against the grain" of what has been done or what *man* may be telling you to do because it opposes the *rhema* word of God. There is nothing wrong with wisdom from counselors. It is needed, but I feel strongly for 2020 and beyond that there is going to be a mighty separation of God's wisdom from man's wisdom and a line drawn in the sand for the body of Christ to choose whom they will follow—God or man. Psalm 119:112 will be one of the key scriptures for 2020 and beyond:

> *I have determined in my heart to obey whatever you say, fully and forever!* (TPT)

In 2020, the heart of God requires His people to make a determined decision of the heart and decree of the mouth to *fully obey* and trust the Lord and the revelation of His ways. For the Lord is going to lead His people deeper into the revelation and manifestation of Psalm 16:6-11 in 2020 and beyond:

> *Your pleasant path leads me to pleasant places. I'm overwhelmed by the privileges that come with following you, for you have given me the best! The way you counsel and correct me makes me praise you more, for your whispers in the night give me wisdom, showing me what to do next. Because you are close to me and always available, my confidence will never be shaken, for I experience your wrap-around presence every moment. My heart and soul explode with joy—full of glory! Even my body will rest confident and secure. For you will not*

*abandon me to the realm of death, nor will you allow
your Holy One to experience corruption. For you bring
me a continual revelation of resurrection life, the path
to the bliss that brings me face-to-face with you* (TPT).

Wholehearted obedience to the Lord even in the unexpected, "going against the grain" in what doesn't seem to make sense in the natural—that type of faith in His Word and trust in His wisdom will position the people of God for demonstrations of His power, miracles, and partnership with His Spirit. We will see Heaven come to earth and the glory and majesty of God unveiled in the earth in a way we have never seen before. All of Heaven will back the obedience of God's people. The favor, the provision, the weight of His glory and hand of God upon and through the lives of those who will obey will be astounding. The Lord is coming in power. We have known Him as the Lamb; He is now coming as the Lion in this new era. He whispered to me recently, "Ready or not, here I come." Our obedience, humility, and yielding to His ways is a place of preparation and making ourselves ready for the King of glory to come (see Ps. 24:7-9).

The modern-day Noahs are arising in this new era and we will see more and more of them rising up in 2020 and beyond. They have heard the Word of the Lord and obey no matter the cost. They obey fully and completely what the Lord has said.

The Lord is looking for those in 2020 and beyond to whom He can entrust the secrets and wisdom of His heart, who will engage with Him and His ways fully and build with Him in His way and strategy no matter what it looks like. From this place, cities will be changed. Nations will be impacted. Families will be transformed; major demonstrations of His power will be seen, and moves of His Spirit bringing rapid and radical reformation will be demonstrated in significant ways. The Lord is extending the invitation to all, but it is our responsibility to make ourselves ready through our faith, our humility, our obedience, and yielding to His ways.

THE FEAR OF MAN UPROOTED

In this year of *bold* and *courageous faith* with explosive demonstrations of His power, the fear of man must be uprooted. This is the place of building and running with Him like we have never seen before, a mighty wind of empowerment upon the saints of God to do what we never thought we could do and go where we never thought we would go with Him.

There will be *mighty* encounters with the Lord in 2020 and beyond that, like Isaiah 6, will uproot the fear of man. The revelation of His power, His majesty, and His glory will so consume the people of God with eyes and hearts toward Him that the fear of man will have no place. The love and glory of God will so overtake and overwhelm the people of God that fear of man will have no place, leaving them and the Church trembling in awe before Him.

These words then thundered around me: *"Many of God's people have feared man and the enemy rather than living in the fear of God. Now is the time for the people of God to be restored into the place of wonder and awe of God. The fear of God restored will uproot the fear of man once and for all."*

There will be a divine transaction that will take place in 2020. Where many have trembled at the enemy and trembled at the thought of others' opinions or approval/rejection, the powerful restoration of the fear of God to the Church will cause them to tremble at the holiness of God and the awe of God and His power. This will then raise up a people who answer the call of the Lord *"Who will go for us?"* with a reply of *"Here I am, Lord, send me."* A place of *yes* and answering the call no matter what it looks like.

The Lord didn't give Isaiah the ten-step plan and then say, "Will you go for Me?" The heart of God called him to partner with Him, and because of the revelation of His majesty, His holiness, His greatness, Isaiah was left undone and completely changed. His vision shifted from seeing his sinfulness to seeing the glory of God. He was marked, branded, changed forever, and the fruit of this encounter was a *yes* to God and a commissioning. Brian Simmons states in his commentary notes on Isaiah 6:8 in *The Passion Translation:* "No prophet or servant of the Lord answered God's call more swiftly than Isaiah."

In 2020 and beyond, the fear of God will be restored to the Church. The holiness of God and a wave of holiness will be restored to the Church. A fire of purging and purifying will continue to blaze through the Church bringing forth a purity in the hearts and lives of believers, bringing the people of God into a greater place of preparation to partner with Him in what He is going to do in the earth. It's not about being perfect; it's about being positioned and available. Yielded.

You Will See What You Decree

You will decide on a matter, and it will be established for you, and light will shine on your ways (Job 22:28).

You will also decide and decree a thing, and it will be established for you; and the light [of God's favor] will shine upon your ways (Job 22:28 AMP).

There is a weighty fear of the Lord and sense of urgency in a glorious way that I feel on 2020 in what we speak. Part of the bold faith that the Lord is inviting us to walk in, in 2020 and beyond, is aligning our mouths with what the Lord is revealing. 2020 will see a greater clarity come to hearing the voice of God and seeing what He sees as we seek Him. There is an invitation into alignment in 2020 to rise up in decreeing what He sees, and there will then be greater accelerated powerful demonstrations of the manifestation of His Word in the lives of believers.

As God raises up a people in faith, in the revelation of the power of the Word of God and the power of the mustard seed, decreeing what He is saying, there will be a divine *establishment* of the Word in profound ways in 2020 and beyond. That is why God is training His people now to be careful what is on your lips and to speak only what *He* sees. In 2020 and beyond God's people will not only step up into greater authority and revelation of their identity and their seat (see Eph. 2:6) and govern from that place but will actually begin to see accelerated manifestation in the natural what God is seeing and saying. As you decree what He sees in 2020 and beyond, you will see that which He speaks.

We have entered a new era. An era like no other. It's time to be positioned and prepared to see a move of God in our lives, our families, cities, and nations unlike anything we have ever seen.

He's whispering, *"Ready or not, here I come."*

My question and cry is, *"Lord, am I ready? Make me ready."*

Get ready, people of God—mountains are going to shake and be moved in 2020 and beyond as you step up into your identity and authority in Christ, operating in bold faith like you have never seen before and reintroduced to the power of God that will change you forever.

King of Glory! Come!

ABOUT LANA VAWSER

Lana Vawser is first and foremost, a pursuer of God's heart and secondly, a prophetic voice to the nations. Her desire is to help people develop deep intimacy with Jesus and activate their prophetic hearing to recognize God speaking in everyday life. Lana is driven by a vision to see people set free and walking in the abundant life that Jesus purchased for them. She is an itinerant preacher and prophetic revivalist who gets to participate in powerful moves of God throughout the nations. Lana is married to Kevin and they live in Adelaide, Australia, with their three sons.

Chapter 5

Justice and Upgrades: Replacing the Inferior with the Superior

Robert Henderson

2020 will be a year of the replacement of the inferior with the superior. It will be a year of the partial being replaced with the full. It will be a year of the less being replaced with the more. God will be upgrading His people into new realms of influence and empowerment for the days we live in. We see this being prophesied in several different places, but especially in the book of Isaiah. Isaiah 55:13 declares that we will see places that curses rule become places of blessings being expressed and known.

> *Instead of the thorn shall come up the cypress tree, and instead of the brier shall come up the myrtle tree; and it shall be to the Lord for a name, for an everlasting sign that shall not be cut off* (NKJV).

Thorns and briars always speak of the curse. This goes all the way back to when a curse came on Adam and Eve and creation as a result of their rebellion and disobedience. Genesis 3:17-19 expresses that thorns and thistles are signs of the curse.

> *Then to Adam He said, "Because you have heeded the voice of your wife, and have eaten from the tree of which I commanded you, saying, 'You shall not eat of it':*
>
> *"Cursed is the ground for your sake; in toil you shall eat of it all the days of your life. Both thorns and thistles it shall bring forth for you, and you shall eat the herb of the field. In the sweat of your face you shall eat bread till you return to the ground, for out of it you were taken; for dust you are, and to dust you shall return"* (NKJV).

Several things were associated with this curse. One of the main things was *diminished returns* from labor. In other words, they would work hard but produce little from their efforts. Their work would bring forth thorns and thistles rather than fruit bearing produce. I decree that 2020 will be the year of *instead!* Instead of thorns and briars there will be fruitfulness. Myrtle and cypress trees will be produced rather than thorns and thistles. The cypress tree represents certain very powerful biblical principles.

Physicians frequently sent patients with lung disorders and difficulty breathing to the isle of Crete, where cypress trees grow. Biblically, the cypress tree stands tall too. In the Christian tradition, the cypress is a symbol of death, life, and resurrection, and it signifies the heavens calling.

When God declares that *instead cypress* will grow, He is declaring that His breath, life, and Spirit will resuscitate and bring into resurrection that which has died or is close to dying. *Instead* of 2020 being a time of death, despair, discouragement, and disillusionment, it will be a time of resurrection from the dead through the breath of God's Spirit bringing renewal, resuscitation, and even revival. We are in the place of God replacing and upgrading!

The myrtle tree also is important. The myrtle tree replaces the briars just like the cypress replaces the thorns. The myrtle tree is easily traced to Queen Esther who was pivotal in saving the Jews from destruction because of the wicked plans of Haman. Queen Esther's birth name was Hadassah, which means *myrtle* in Hebrew—a flowering plant native to the Mediterranean region. The myrtle is known for its leaves, which release their *fragrance* only when they are crushed.

Just like Hadassah/Esther became a savior to the nation of Israel, God is raising up saviors in this day as well. We know there is only one Savior, Jesus Christ. Yet God also promises to raise deliverers from Zion, the place of His presence. Obadiah 1:21 promises that *saviors* will come to judge and set in order that an expression of the kingdom of God might be seen.

> *Then saviors shall come to Mount Zion to judge the mountains of Esau, and the kingdom shall be the Lord's* (NKJV).

The Savior, Jesus Christ, will have those who walk in the same Spirit and authority that He walks in. There will be those who will be *saviors* even as Hadassah/Esther was to her people. Through the fragrance they carry as the people of God, they shall free people into destiny and purpose. The crushing they went through and endured will allow the fragrances of Heaven to saturate their lives. They shall operate in the Courts of Heaven as judges. Their function in this dimension will cause the myrtle tree and its aroma and fragrance to see salvation and deliverance come to a generation of people. There will be a deliverance from bondage into the glorious liberty of the children of God.

Another place we see God replacing that which has been with a higher order is Isaiah 60:17. We are promised an increase and an enlargement from that which has been.

> *Instead of bronze I will bring gold, instead of iron I will bring silver, instead of wood, bronze, and instead of stones, iron. I will also make your officers peace, and your magistrates righteousness* (NKJV).

This scripture implies and declares an increase and upgrade in all things. It is speaking of going from that which is inferior, even though good, to that which is superior that is the better and best. The Lord even promises that those who are leaders over us will operate in a greater realm of His heart. They will not be abusive but will provide a place of safety and motivation that is positive and not negative. The word *peace* is the word *shalom* in the Hebrew and means safety, well, happy, friendly, and good welfare. So our officers and those whom we answer to create this kind of environment for work, function, and life. The word *magistrate* is the Hebrew word *naga* and it means a workman who tyrannizes. It means to harass and to drive.

It is speaking of those who seek to motivate through oppression and fear. God says that in this new season of upgrade the heart of those you work under and function with will change. God will grant you people to work with and under that will be people of peace and righteousness. Even this will be upgraded.

The Lord promises upgrades even in life. Jesus declared in John 10:10 that He came that we might have life and have it abundantly. It's one thing to have life. It's another thing to have abundant life.

> *The thief does not come except to steal, and to kill, and to destroy. I have come that they may have life, and that they may have it more abundantly.*

In 2020, God desires to upgrade us into the abundant life and not just life. The word *abundantly* is the Greek word *perissos,* and it means that which is beyond and superior. It means to be super abundant. Jesus comes to break every power of the thief and restore back to us what has been stolen. We are upgraded into life from the thievery of the devil. The Lord doesn't stop there. He wants to upgrade us into that which is beyond and superior. We are to have the life that is beyond imagination. I was on the set of a television show recently. The host of this show is an older person in the body of Christ. As I sat on the sofa readying myself for the interview, this person said to me, *"I didn't know you could be this happy."* It was a genuine expression of the life of God flowing through them. Their life had not been perfect. Of their own admission there had been depression and difficulty in early years. There had been the loss of a greatly loved spouse. Yet here they sat at this stage in life declaring their happiness and amazement at the goodness of God. This is the *abundant life.* God desires to bring each of us into this place of upgrade.

I am reminded of 1 Peter 3:10-12. We are told a prescription for living this kind of life.

> *He who would love life and see good days, let him refrain his tongue from evil, and his lips from speaking deceit. Let him turn away from evil and do good; let him seek peace and pursue it. For the eyes of the Lord are on the righteous, and His ears are open to their prayers; but the face of the Lord is against those who do evil* (NKJV).

If we are to *love our life, and experience good days,* we should 1) pause our tongue from hurtful speech, 2) not be untruthful and/or crafty with our words, 3) forsake evil, 4) do good instead, 5) seek only the things that create peace in our hearts and with others. The Bible says when we do these things God's eyes are on us and He listens to our prayers. We are promised an upgrade into abundant life when we conduct ourselves in these ways.

The Bible mentions another upgrade in Isaiah 61:7-9. We are told that the shame and confusion we have experienced will be replaced with honor and great joy and rejoicing.

> *Instead of your shame you shall have double honor, and instead of confusion they shall rejoice in their portion. Therefore in their land they shall possess double; everlasting joy shall be theirs. "For I, the Lord, love justice; I hate robbery for burnt offering; I will direct their work in truth, and will make with them an everlasting covenant. Their descendants shall be known among the Gentiles, and their offspring among the people. All who see them shall acknowledge them, that they are the posterity whom the Lord has blessed"* (NKJV).

We are promised double honor and joy for every shame and confusion we have experienced. The reason for this is because God loves justice. In other words, it is the justice of God that will repay you with double for any and all unrighteous treatment you have experienced. 2020 will be a year of the justice and judgement of God in your favor. It will not just be for you but also for your children after you. The Word promises that the offspring will be acknowledged as the ones God has blessed. This will be a result of the covenant we have with the Lord.

My family and I are no foreigners to shame and confusion. We walked through a very difficult season when great lies were told about me. In the place where these lies were told and believed, I wanted nothing to do with it. God had other plans. One night I had a dream. In the dream the one who had perhaps told the lies but at the least promoted them came to me. He had within his hand a legal document. He wanted me to sign it. If I signed the document, I was signing away my rights to this particular place and city. However, I wasn't just signing away my rights; I was signing away my children's rights as well. When I awoke I readily knew God was cautioning me. Even though at the time I had nothing but painful memories from and about that place, God was letting me know a portion of my children and my inheritance was there. I was not to give up those rights nor *sign* them away. I was to exercise my rights that God said I had, to reclaim double honor and joy where there had been shame and confusion.

This is what we had and are doing. Houses and property that were ripped from our hands have been restored. Every effort to destroy us and our reputation has been negated. Instead of pain and hurt in this place, there is now increasing joy and pleasure. God loves to take the places of pain and produce pleasure from them. We believe that instead of shame there will be increasing double honor. Instead of confusion there will be great rejoicing. This is because we serve the God of redemption and reclamation. 2020 is a year of the upgrades of the Lord into a fuller expression of destiny and future! Our God as Judge loves *justice!*

ABOUT ROBERT HENDERSON

Robert Henderson is a global apostolic leader who operates in revelation and impartation. His teaching empowers the body of Christ to see the hidden truths of Scripture clearly and apply them for breakthrough results. Driven by a mandate to disciple nations through writing and speaking, Robert travels extensively around the globe, teaching on the apostolic, the Kingdom of God, the "Seven Mountains" and most notably, the Courts of Heaven. He has been married to Mary for 40 years. They have six children and five grandchildren. Together they are enjoying life in beautiful Waco, TX.

Chapter 6

THE CHRIST-CONFIGURED CHURCH AND THE DEMONIAC NATIONS

David Balestri

This prophetic word is a collaboration between David Balestri, some the prophetic company team leaders from Hope Unlimited church that he leads, and also a company of national and global apostolic leaders with whom he walks in alignment.

The Gerasene Demoniac

They came to the other side of the sea, into the country of the Gerasenes. When He got out of the boat, immediately a man from the tombs with an unclean spirit met Him, and he had his dwelling among the tombs. And no one was able to bind him anymore, even with a chain; because he had often been bound with shackles and chains, and the chains had been torn apart by him and the shackles broken in pieces, and no one was strong enough to subdue him. Constantly, night and day, he was screaming among the tombs and in the mountains and gashing himself with stones. Seeing Jesus from a distance, he ran up and bowed down before Him; and shouting with a loud voice, he said, "What business do we have with each other, Jesus, Son of the Most High God? I implore You by God, do not torment me!" For He had been saying to him, "Come out of the man, you unclean spirit!" And He was asking him, "What is your name?" And he said to Him, "My name is Legion; for we are many." And he began to implore Him earnestly not to send them out of the country. Now there was a large herd of swine feeding nearby on the mountain. The demons implored Him, saying, "Send us into the swine so that we may enter them." Jesus gave them permission. And coming out, the unclean spirits entered the swine; and the herd rushed down the steep bank into the sea, about two thousand of them; and they were drowned in the sea.

Their herdsmen ran away and reported it in the city and in the country. And the people came to see what it was that had happened. They came to Jesus and observed the man who had been demon-possessed sitting down, clothed and in his right mind, the very man who had had the "legion"; and they became frightened. Those who had seen it described to them how it had happened to the demon-possessed man, and all about the swine. And they began to implore Him to leave their region. As He was getting into the boat, the man who had been demon-possessed was imploring Him that he might accompany Him. And He did not let him, but He said to him, "Go home to your people and report to them what great things the Lord has done for you, and how He had mercy on you." And he went away and began to proclaim in Decapolis what great things Jesus had done for him; and everyone was amazed (Mark 5:1-20 NASB).*

PROPHETIC IMPRESSIONS

The church is in the midst of a major culture war in the nations with demonically inspired strongmen.

There is a new era of expression coming upon the body of Christ.

Just as Jesus went outside of His dominant focus at that time (which was the Jewish people) and began to engage into Gentile areas!

The Church's eyes are being refocused toward the transformation of our cities and nations, not just our church structures.

An assignment of death has been stirred up against the nations in this hour. The assignment is not simply a physical war, but also a mind war that has become animated and emboldened.

A passion for the deliverance of our cities and nations is being stirred deep within the hearts of many in the body of Christ in this hour, provoking a boldness of confrontational love.

Even today, the political systems in the nations have begun to lose their illusions about their own ability to keep a grip on this seeming prevailing darkness.

The immediate days ahead will continue their progression toward even greater unrest and upheaval in many major cities of the earth.

The nations are in the torment of anxiety and depression under this constant assault, with seemingly no one in sight to deliver them

The cry of the nations will pull the vanguard leaders in the body of Christ toward aligning with God's strategic plans for His Kingdom purposes to be outworked

The church configured into the position of Christ will draw the attention of the nations. (The disciples had just experienced a massive upgrade in their revelation of Jesus, from anointed teacher to one who has authority over the created order, at the end of Mark 4.)

This infestation of the works of darkness in our culture is multifaceted and integrated deeply (Legion).

It will require an encounter with a church that is configured to Christ and His throne to unhinge this spiritual bondage in the nations.

There will be an exposure in the body of Christ as to who is ready to answer this opportunity to bring the Lordship of Christ, and also who is not ready due to building with lethargy and compromise in the last season.

Jesus exposes the ultimate assignment of this demonic cluster by allowing them to enter the swine. Immediately, their agenda of destruction is exposed.

We have an agenda dominantly expressed in the earth that values the created order of everything else above human life. Jesus shows that one human life made in the image of God is God's priority over all other forms of life.

There will be a realignment of the value of human life above all other forms of created order again.

As the Christ-configured church emerges to bring deliverance from this systematic delusion in the nations, some nations will still position themselves in an adversarial position toward the church and continue down their path of oppression and destruction, as the swine experienced.

Some of the nations that currently carry the darkest light will be turned toward the Lord and become massive missionary-sending centers in the days to come.

2020 PROPHETIC TRIGGERS

Body of Christ

The activation of Christians in the marketplace will accelerate greatly, with unusual favor being placed upon key people in the nations, surprising many with their acknowledgment of Christ (many more Kanyes).

There will be a mighty surge of believers activated in the marketplace who are retooled with unusual wisdom and insight for their spheres of assignment, challenging many of the churches in their traditional understanding of mission expression.

The migration from institutional affiliations to relational family alignments will cause a reshuffling of many in the church. This will cause the dismantling and also the shutting down of some movements in the body of Christ who have abandoned the faith or who have failed to migrate to the Holy Spirit's leading over the last several decades.

The growing understanding of apostolic and prophetic ministry will continue to change the operational landscape of the body of Christ, with many movements who were initially skeptical and resistant to this reality shifting slowly into a more embracive position.

Nations

There will be a swinging back to more conservative social policies in nations that have been seen as front runners for more progressive ideals. I see eastern European nations swinging back—Poland, Ukraine, Latvia were names that I heard.

America will continue to surge forward economically and socially. I see a nation coming and creating a great provocation toward the US. It will be a front, as the real power nation behind this nation will be looking to try and distract the US so that it can gain economic advantage (a bear standing behind a green snake).

I see escalated violence in the US in the lead up to the 2020 presidential election. I see a potential explosion attack in a crowded rally in Washington; however, I see prayer warriors forming a circle around the potential incident site. I believe that a united prayer movement in the lead up to these elections will create a hedge of protection that will thwart many, if not all of these types of incidents.

A consortium of Christ-fearing global leaders will form behind the scenes, and a global thrust of ethical and godly rulership will be forged. Many policies will be scripted that will marry Kingdom values, though these will not be written with overtly Christian language. This will drive the news media wild with conspiracy theory stories being propagated.

Economies

The stock market will continue to rise in 2020 globally and will land stronger by the end of the year.

I hear medicine, money, and minerals as the standout investments in 2020.

A war of financial terrorism will continue amongst the economically stronger nations against the weaker ones. Africa will continue to suffer this pillaging, as its internal corruptions will cause them to not be able to rally properly against these attacks.

China will regroup itself after its battle with the US and look to recoup its financial losses from other nations. Government leaders will need to choose their alliances well to build a buffer against this "red invasion"!

ABOUT DAVID BALESTRI

David serves as an executive leader and business manager at Hope Unlimited Church located on the Central Coast of Sydney in Australia, under Senior Pastors Mark and Darlene Zschech.

David also functions at a trans-local level as a prophet to several apostolic networks and travels extensively around the globe as an advocate of the apostolic and prophetic ministry paradigm that is being restored into the body of Christ at this time.

David is recognized as a governmental building prophet to the body of Christ and works with senior pastors, networks and denominations in building functional prophetic architecture and strategies for the extension of the kingdom in the context of local church.

Chapter 7

A Time of Purification and Pieces Coming Together

Ana Werner

There before me I could see the gates of Heaven.

Recently, I was taken up into a vision, and I heard as I was entering into this encounter: "2020."

I found myself looking down on a scene from what seemed like a bird's-eye view. There before me was the most beautiful Bride. She was radiating light, her gown seemed to glisten with diamonds, and she was smiling and looking forward. The Bride was just breathtaking and gorgeous. Then I was taken to see what she was looking at from her viewpoint. Right before her were the most beautiful set of golden gates. As I looked, what surprised me was that the entrance to pass through the gates was quite narrow.

I saw the Bride smile as she passed through and entered the gates.

The year 2020, I believe, will be the most purifying year the Body of Christ has yet to see. God is setting a bar or standard for us all to live a more righteous and holy life. The purity of the Bride was what I was captivated by, and also the narrow entrance to the gate.

Many of us may think "purity" and shudder at the thought, but I believe it is actually something worth celebrating. God is preparing us for the greatest outpouring of His glory and Presence that we have yet to see. While I know the veil has been torn and we are not living in Old Testament times, there is something to be said about the purification process the priests would go through before entering into the Holy of Holies. Perhaps the Lord is preparing us by purification.

> *Aaron and his sons shall wash their hands and their feet from it; when they enter the tent of meeting, they shall wash with water, so that they will not die; or when they approach the altar to minister, by offering up in smoke a fire sacrifice to the Lord* (Exodus 30:19-20 NASB).

What Does Purification Look Like?

Purification with Our Purpose

This is a time when God is bringing many of us back to our first love—*Jesus!* Do you remember when you first fell in love with Him? You would do anything for Him, give anything to Him, simply because you loved Him. This call for laid-down lovers changes the way our purpose and/or ministry looks entirely. Isn't it wonderful that we aren't workers for Jesus but lovers. By pursuing our first call to love Him, fruit will come out of the overflow of our relationship with Him. As He purifies our purpose, healthy and whole ministers of the Gospel will come forth who are truly rooted and grounded in the love of God (see Eph. 3:17). The Lord is dealing with the healing and restoration of our hearts right now in this moment. There's this invitation from the Father. He says, "Come up here and get your identity wrapped up in Me first, before you go and pour out." Many of us need to lean on His chest and have Him speak back to us who we are. "This is who you are. This is who I've created you to be!" Our "why" is getting clarified! This is *why* I do what I do—out of love for Him.

Righteousness and Turning Away from Sin

I have felt strongly in my spirit that many hidden sins will be brought to light in this hour. Although this process is painful, it is actually a positive thing. It will bring a mature Bride who won't stand for compromise. God is calling us up higher.

> *Who may ascend into the hill of the Lord? And who may stand in His holy place? He who has clean hands and a pure heart* (Psalm 24:3-4 NASB).

Righteousness is not a bad word, although perhaps old language brings a picture to mind of someone who is prideful or self-righteous, putting themselves up on a pedestal. That's not the case at all! No, no! The level of righteousness I'm talking about are worshipers who want to look more and more like Jesus, who are willing to go to God in desperation knowing how much we *need* Him, and who will repent and walk away from sin. The more we long for Him, the more we want to look like Him and turn away from the things that do not look like Him. Someday, we will all stand before God and there will be a storyline played of our lives, and we will have to take everything into account. This is the season when mature ministers of the gospel will come forth.

Breakthrough Is Now!

When I saw the Bride walk through those gates, although they were narrow, she passed through. This brought me so much encouragement and it should for you too! Many of us have felt like we have been in a narrow place this past year. We have been pressing and pushing through trying times and at some points what felt like a real time of testing of our faith. Out of that wine press comes the purest of wine! It's been a season of real refinement and testing, but we are passing through to the other side. Isn't that encouraging!

I am declaring over you right now that you are walking toward Jesus; you are through with the season of pressing and are now walking into the new. It's turning the page of the next chapter in your story. Those who have felt stuck I am declaring to be unstuck. Forgive me for the lack of profound wording, but you are *unstuck* and walking through to victory.

Wave of Glory Coming

I believe we are in a constant state of being present with the King of kings, but there is a wave of His glory coming to the earth that will overpower the dominion of darkness. Yes, darkness on the earth is great right now, *but God*, I repeat, *but God* is pouring out His Presence and about to release angels on assignment and ambassadors for His Kingdom to ambush the plans and schemes of the enemy. This outpouring will be the greatest outpouring the world has yet seen. I've seen it. The Lord took me in a vision when I was back in Israel, and I saw a timeline in history as I looked into the eyes of Jesus. I saw what looked like a tsunami wave of glory crashing over the entire earth and it carried fire in it. As it hit, I saw masses of people running to the altars in repentance and crying out for Jesus. I am convinced that this purification process the Lord is about to take us through as the Body of Christ is setting us all up for the greatest harvest of souls!

THE PIECES COMING TOGETHER

As a seer, the Lord mostly speaks to me prophetically through the gift of seeing images or pictures. Through these visions, the Lord speaks to me and downloads revelations to me.

I was in my car one day driving (imagine getting a prophetic picture with your eyes wide open overlaid on top of the street your seeing in front of your dashboard!) and God showed me a picture and spoke the number "2020."

I saw what looked like a giant puzzle with all these brightly colored pieces. I watched as the pieces were all coming together, piece by piece. Then suddenly there was a giant shift, almost like someone took the playing board and nudged its position in a different direction. That shift caused all the pieces then to click together in place.

I believe 2020 is the year when we will finally be stepping into what is we are called to do. Many of us will stand back and have these "Ah-ha" moments as things finally come together. Projects we have been working on, business promotions, stepping into your niche for ministry, right alignments, even things within the family structure—basically things that seemed difficult or full or striving before, suddenly there will be a *great shift* and things are going to fall into place with ease. You will look back and think, *God was setting me up for this all along,* and will be able to see back through memory lane over your life at how the Lord's hand was gently leading and nudging you all along. You will be stepping into your calling all the more. You will experience that thrill of "this is what I was made for!" as your passion and your natural, God-given abilities and unique gifting mix will shine.

I see many people picking up old dreams that were once set aside and pursuing them again but with better clarity and direction now. God is bringing clarity to our vision, direction, and purpose in 2020. What you declare even over yourself in this season is also so important, as this also is the year when God is highlighting the mouth. Declarations that match the vision God has given you will bring things to pass that previously felt like they were not gaining any momentum. You will be stepping into what you are supposed to be doing.

As well, when I saw the pieces click into place, I felt in my spirit, "Right alignment clicking into place." In this year, look to correct your relationships or alignments that will promote or propel you forward. Right leadership will fall into place and also accountability. Leadership and accountability are so key, especially for us pioneers. As we go take on the world, it's so wonderful to have someone there to pull back the reigns a bit and say, "Hey there, have you thought about this?" or "How's your heart doing with this?" Right alliances are also so important. As I look at my daughter now (who is only six) and wonder about what it will be like to parent her as a teenager, I think about how important it is to know who her friends are who carry influence in her life. In the same way, we want to be rightly aligned with people who speak into our lives with authority, who hold us accountable, who encourage us in our calling and push us when we need stretching, and who are running in the same direction—passionately toward *Jesus!* So, who is influencing you in this season the most?

PRAYER

God, I love You. Thank You for Your goodness. Thank You for calling me Your son, Your daughter, even despite my own weakness. Jesus, I pray, help me Lord. I need You God. God, You know I'm a sinner and I'm not perfect. God, I repent for my sins and ask You for Your forgiveness. Help me to be more like You each day to the world around me, Jesus.

God, I thank You now that finally I am getting clarity on what it is that I'm supposed to be doing with You. Although many opportunities may arise, I only want what You have for me. Help me to only commit to what You have shown me is mine to take on. Thank You for the clarity and the direction You are giving me.

God, I pray that You would now remove any obstacle that keeps me from moving forward. Thank You, Papa, that I am unstuck and I have forward momentum. This is the season for me to rise up and pick up my old dreams. Dreams that I have had really all my life, but now seem to make sense. May You breathe life on them again. Help me have courage, God. Give me vision, Lord. Give me direction. May You have all the glory, Lord. Keep me humble. Keep me pure.

Amen.

ABOUT ANA WERNER

Ana Werner and her husband Sam reside in Missouri with their two beautiful children, and are the associate directors of the Heartland Healing Rooms in Lees Summit. Ana travels internationally and equips people to see in the Spirit, move in the prophetic, and experience healing and deliverance through her ministry. Her transparency as she shares the realities and experiences she has had in Heaven, brings the Holy Spirit, the love of the Father, and the power of God into the room when she speaks. Ana is passionate about leading people into encountering Jesus' heart.

For more information visit: anawerner.org

Chapter 8

THE DECADE OF DIFFERENCE

Hank and Brenda Kunneman

RIDICULOUS, EXPOSE

"Listen," says the Spirit of God, "seasons come, seasons go, and seasons change. I say this because those who have ears to hear and eyes to see shall surely see that something unusual is taking place. Something has shifted, and a new era has arisen upon you, and I speak to this nation of the United States. There is a new season upon you and as this new season manifests I must show you that which is ridiculous and that which I am humored by; therefore, as you see this spring, this summer, your fall into next year 2020, watch the ridiculous things that shall arise that you will say, 'Is this true? Is this for real? This is ridiculous!' Watch your headlines, for they will bear witness when they will say, 'Ridiculous. Ridiculous. Ridiculous.' Why is this? Because I am stepping in now and I'm showing this nation the ridiculous agenda of those who think they can push Me and My name out of this nation. I'm going to expose, expose, expose now at another level and there will be those who will say, 'This is ridiculous.'"

Decade of Difference: Movement, Dividing in Party

God says, "What shall you do when mothers and fathers and families, not too far in your distant future, shall say 'Let us have a movement and a march that joins the family and brings our children and our sons and daughters to declare great is our God!' and they shall gather from the north and the south and the east and the west and your media shall not be able to contain or handle this side that they say have been hostile."

God says, "They do not march in hostility; they march to the God of wonder, to the God of power, and to the God of might who has come to embrace 2020 and to what shall begin in 2020 as a new decade. I've said to you that it shall be known and declared as the decade of difference. I say this because things shall shift! And things will be different, especially for those who have called upon My name. I am the same God who caused Pharaoh to say, 'Who is this that you say shall do these things?' Yet I put a difference in the land of Egypt and of the land of My people Israel, and I brought a distinction. This is what this decade shall be known by, and the leaders of this land who have mocked and tried to push Me out and who have tried in their pride to build something without Me, like the days of Babel, I shall cause a dividing to come to them and even to their party. Enough! Enough of those who say this nation shall be without God."

DECADE OF DIFFERENCE: THUMBPRINT

God says, "You have not just entered into 2020 but you've entered into a decade that shall be known as a decade of difference. What do I mean?" The Spirit of God says, "Remember where I declared in My Word I will put a difference and there shall be light in Goshen but it shall be dark in Egypt. Certain plagues and things would not touch the place of Goshen because I put a difference.

"I speak this to you who have fallen into a place of despair, a place of fear. What you shall enter into in this new decade will start off harsh, but it shall come to a place known as rest and it shall be different. And I will do this, foolish as you may think as you hear this, to confound those who think they are wise with their instruments of weather, their almanacs, their global warming; and they will say, 'We don't understand,' but you're not supposed to because I am the God who has My hand upon the thumbprint and the heartbeat of this land, and I'm walking among it through the cities and the territories and the regions to bring about great change. Do not be afraid, for you have been through floods and you've seen the fires, and now you shall come into the season when your soil will shake. Don't be afraid, for when the soil shook in the days of the crucified Christ it was because of what was being resurrected. I am raising you up, United States," says the Spirit of God.

2020–2032: REST, PROTEST, REVOLUTION OF LIGHT

One of the things that the Lord has promised in the new era, and I saw it (in a vision) on February 12, 2019, and the meteorologists were on, and it was a future time, and it wasn't too far in the distance when the weather person was forecasting major hurricanes and all of a sudden, they said at the end of the season, "We don't understand this, that there have not been the things we've predicted." And I saw, on February 12, 2019, the Lord showed me 2020–2032, I'm not setting dates, and if the Lord shall tarry these are things He desires to bring. And the Lord told me He only let me see that far in the future because He said I couldn't handle more. And I heard these words:

> "I will bring rest to the land of the United States that will even affect the weather patterns, that shall affect the schools where there shall be prayer implemented again for the children shall rise up and they shall say, 'We want to pray to our Father in Heaven in Jesus' name; we want to join hands and read the Scriptures and pray.' They will gather in the streets where there have been protests and violence. The children and college age students shall begin to gather in the streets (as you see in China) for it will continue in China where they will sing unto the Lord and that which is underground shall begin to come above ground. That in the United States that needs to come and begin to shine as part of a movement of a revolution of light, it's coming, and the streets, the malls, the universities shall begin to have an invasion of those who will call out unto God and they will worship and there will be a sound of *great is our God* across the land. This is about to happen, for this land is coming, as I gave rest," says the Spirit of God, "in the days when Joseph was in the place who spoke to his God but spoke to the king of Egypt and spoke to the nation and brought forth the wisdom that brought the land into rest." And so God says, "This is My plan to

bring this nation into rest, but I need My people to unite now," says the Lord.

BRENDA KUNNEMAN: SEASON OF TIME

"And so even now," says the Spirit, "in the hour and the season a time in history when the ground is as shifting sand and things seem unstable, things seem unyielding, and it would seem as though the world around you is coming to crash down, but," the Spirit says, "did not My Word already declare that if you build your house upon the rock, if you build your house upon the Kingdom, though the sands move, though the waters and the floods come, and though the winds blow, did I not already declare in My Word that you shall not be moved? You shall not be shaken and you shall be shown to stand strong and stable. So it is even in this time for I am bringing My church to a place of prominence where they will stand upon the rock even in this nation and in the nations of the world.

"For though it would seem that persecution has heated up and it has been turned up, watch now what I do with My national leaders and those who are called by My name, for they shall rise to a place of celebration and confidence and prominence in this hour. For think not that the enemy has the upper hand, for I am raising My church to the high place in this season!" says the Spirit of God.

ABOUT HANK AND BRENDA KUNNEMAN

Hank Kunneman pastors Lord of Hosts Church in Omaha, Nebraska, with his wife, Brenda. Together they host a weekly program, *New Level* with Hank and Brenda, on *Daystar Television Network*. As an author and uncompromising voice for God's Word, he is known for a strong prophetic anointing, preaching and ministering in meetings and on national television programs. His ministry has truly been marked for accuracy in national and worldwide events.

Brenda Kunneman pastors Lord of Hosts Church, in Omaha, Nebraska, with her husband, Hank. She is a writer and teacher, who ministers nationally and internationally, seeing lives change through the prophetic word and ministry in the Holy Spirit, coupled with a balanced, relevant message. Together, she and her husband also host a weekly TV program, New Level with Hank and Brenda, on Daystar Television Network.

Chapter 9

THE DAYS OF ELIJAH

Patricia King

In the last decade the Holy Spirit emphasized the "eye." During that decade there was a great deal of teaching and focus on subjects such as dreams, interpretation of dreams, visions, trances, and visual encounters. In the coming decade, the Holy Spirit is emphasizing the "mouth." Voice will be given to the Lord's prophets in this hour to address many things that need to come into "righteous alignment."

In Elijah's day, the people of God were ruled by the evil king Ahab, who was more evil than his fathers before him (see 1 Kings 16:30). He married Jezebel (the daughter of a Sidonian king), and became a Baal worshiper. He erected an altar for Baal (a sexual deity) and made the Asherah (a wooden symbol of a female deity; see 1 Kings 16:31).

The nation of Israel compromised their faith and for the most part followed their leaders, although there were seven thousand prophets who had not bowed their knee to Baal (see 1 Kings 19:18). The nation had turned against the Lord through idolatrous compromise. God's prophets had become prophets (voices) for Baal. A prophet is a spokesman for a deity. God's uncompromised prophets in that day were silent—where was their voice?

The days in which Elijah lived are not that different from our day. On a worldwide scale, we find "sexual deities" boldly and unashamedly at work. Displays of promiscuity, perversion, sexual confusion, and "child sacrifice" are establishing anti-biblical values and mindsets in the masses through saturating media, arts and entertainment, and education systems. Governments are passing laws to support such doctrines and sectors of the Christian church have chosen to be a "voice" for such atrocities. We are threatened by "powers that be" to be silent in order to be "politically correct." Yes, the days we live in are very similar to the days of Elijah.

GOD NEEDS A VOICE

In Elijah's day, there were prophets of the Lord in the land, but they were mute. However, God did have a man with a voice who stood fearlessly in the midst of all as His representative. Elijah single-handedly called 450 prophets of Baal to a confrontation on Mount Carmel and challenged them to no longer "hesitate between two opinions" (see 1 Kings 18:21). They were obviously still believers in God but they had added to their faith and devotion other gods and spiritual beliefs. Mixture is dangerous. God is a jealous God (see Exod. 34:14) and desires pure devotion and worship from His people. Elijah was determined to see the voice and power of God settle the issue and to bring these "prophets" to a place of declaring with absolute certainty who the true God was. The God who answered by fire would be identified as the true God. Elijah took action with unshakable confidence.

> *Elijah came near to all the people and said, "How long will you hesitate between two opinions? If the Lord is God, follow Him; but if Baal, follow him." But the people did not answer him a word. Then Elijah said to the people, "I alone am left a prophet of the Lord, but Baal's prophets are 450 men. Now let them give us two oxen; and let them choose one ox for themselves and cut it up, and place it on the wood, but put no fire under it; and I will prepare the other ox and lay it on the wood, and I will not put a fire under it. Then you call on the name of your god, and I will call on the name of the Lord, and the God who answers by fire, He is God." And all the people said, "That is a good idea"* (1 Kings 18:21-24 NASB).

Everyone agreed on the plan, and Elijah allowed the prophets of Baal to go first. Look at the results:

> *So Elijah said to the prophets of Baal, "Choose one ox for yourselves and prepare it first for you are many, and call on the name of your god, but put no fire under it." Then they took the ox which was given them and they prepared it and called on the name of Baal from morning until noon saying, "O Baal, answer us." But there was no voice and no one answered. And they leaped about the altar which they made. It came about at noon, that Elijah mocked them and said, "Call out*

with a loud voice, for he is a god; either he is occupied or gone aside, or is on a journey, or perhaps he is asleep and needs to be awakened." So they cried with a loud voice and cut themselves according to their custom with swords and lances until the blood gushed out on them. When midday was past, they raved until the time of the offering of the evening sacrifice; but there was no voice, no one answered, and no one paid attention (1 Kings 18:25-29 NASB).

Even though they used their voice to summon their god, there was no response—no voice response and no power response. Have you ever asked yourself why? These prophets of Baal were used to seeing the supernatural and they had every expectation of their god responding in both voice and action. They never would have agreed to Elijah's terms if they had no confidence in their god responding. Why then was there no response from Baal? I believe it was due to Elijah's authoritative presence.

The Body of believers today needs to understand the power we have in Christ. Jesus said, *"Behold, I have given you authority to tread on serpents and scorpions, and over all the power of the enemy, and nothing will injure you"* (Luke 10:19 NASB). He also taught us, *"I will give you the keys of the kingdom of heaven; and whatever you bind on earth shall have been bound in heaven, and whatever you loose on earth shall have been loosed in heaven"* (Matt. 16:19 NASB).

Elijah knew the authority he had as a prophet of the Lord, and that is why he could stay the power of the evil entities of that day in the midst of the confrontation. We need such boldness today. We need to act on the authority we have been given.

Then Elijah called them to carefully observe as he prepared the altar of the Lord that had been torn down. The altar represents the place of pure devotion, offering, and sacrifice. The torn down altar was a sign of the condition of the hearts of God's people. Elijah repaired it. In our day, we need to examine the altars of our faith and devotion—does the altar of our life need repair? Does the altar of the church nationwide need repair?

> *Then Elijah said to all the people, "Come near to me." So all the people came near to him. And he repaired the altar of the Lord which had been torn down. Elijah took twelve stones according to the number of the tribes of the sons of Jacob, to whom the word of the Lord had come, saying, "Israel shall be your name." So with the stones he built an altar in the name of the Lord, and he made a trench around the altar, large enough to hold two measures of seed* (1 Kings 18:30-32 NASB).

After the altar was repaired, he arranged the wood and the sacrifice and then did something amazing: he called for water, and lots of it. This was in a time of drought. Where did the water come from? It might have been from a supernatural source, but for sure it was an offering to the Lord as a seed for the coming rain that would end the drought. Water often symbolizes the Word, the Spirit, and cleansing within the Scripture. Elijah was restoring divine order—Word, Spirit, purity. If there is no divine order, there is no divine glory.

> *Then he arranged the wood and cut the ox in pieces and laid it on the wood. And he said, "Fill four pitchers with water and pour it on the burnt offering and on the wood." And he said, "Do it a second time," and they did it a second time. And he said, "Do it a third time," and they did it a third time. The water flowed around the*

altar and he also filled the trench with water (1 Kings 18:33-35).

What does "restoring order" look like in our day? We first need to examine our own lives. Do we live a mediocre life? Do we love other things, the lusts of the flesh, or the things of the world, more than God? Are we lukewarm in our faith? If so, we need to restore devotion to God alone, offering Him the sacrifice of our lives, giving heed to His Word and Spirit in all things.

What about the church in general? Do we need to set things in order? Have we introduced teachings and concepts that do not support righteous living or encourage pure faith and devotion to Christ? Are we spiritually complacent and compromised? If so, let's call forth order into the church. Let's address these things.

When everything was set in order then Elijah prayed, and God answered.

> *At the time of the offering of the evening sacrifice, Elijah the prophet came near and said, "O Lord, the God of Abraham, Isaac and Israel, today let it be known that You are God in Israel and that I am Your servant and I have done all these things at Your word. Answer me, O Lord, answer me, that this people may know that You, O Lord, are God, and that You have turned their heart back again." Then the fire of the Lord fell and consumed the burnt offering and the wood and the stones and the dust, and licked up the water that was in the trench. When all the people saw it, they fell on their faces; and they said, "The Lord, He is God; the Lord, He is God"* (1 Kings 18:36-39 NASB).

Prayerlessness is possibly one of the church's worst enemies in our day. The Lord is calling His church to much prayer and fasting in order to have much needed breakthrough. The hearts of the people in Elijah's day needed to be turned back to the Lord. This is what he prayed in verse 37 and the Lord responded with a magnificent display of power.

We need the turning of hearts back to the Lord en mass in the world today. God is raising up those in this day who are like Elijah in spirit—uncompromised, fearless, and who are willing to open their mouth and let the Lord fill it. We cannot be silent.

We are living in treacherous times. It is time to align with God, His ways, and His purposes.

On Sunday, October 20, 2019 at 6:00 A.M., the Lord delivered this sobering word to me during my devotion time.

> By great grace and unwavering mercy, I have called My people into My very presence. I have declared and manifest My extravagant goodness to all who are called by My Name. My kindness, My goodness, should have produced repentance unto godliness and greater levels of consecration, but many have denied My call and have turned their hearts away from Me unto their own desires, passions, and lusts. Many have become entitled. Many have allowed their own fleshly and worldly appetites to prevail over their hunger for Me. Many have delighted in sinful ways and declared that I do not see, I do not remember, I do not mind. They have filled their lives with selfish pleasures and have forgotten My covenant. They have willfully continued in sin, justifying their actions, even though they had knowledge

of the truth. They have said, "I am forgiven; grace has covered."

In this hour I will separate the vile from the holy, for My heart has no pleasure in those who choose transgression over Me.

My priests should preserve knowledge, and men should seek instruction from them, but many have been caused to stumble by their deeds. The hearts and actions of many who walk contrary to My ways will be exposed and will no longer be hidden or covered. "Everything hidden and covered up will soon be exposed. For the facade is falling down, and nothing will be kept secret for long. Whatever you have spoken in private will be public knowledge, and what you have whispered secretly behind closed doors will be broadcast far and wide for all to hear" (Luke 12:2-3 TPT). This is a season of exposure, a season of confrontation as I love My people and want them close to My heart.

I am raising up a remnant in this hour who are passionate for Me. They obey Me and allow the power of My grace to establish My righteousness within them and through them. They love Me by keeping My commandments and they pursue My presence, longing to know My ways and to walk in My ways. Through this righteous remnant I will manifest my power and perform great exploits that will turn many to Me.

The world will continue to mock Me and My ways. They will say, "The Bible is not God's Holy Word, for it is simply inspired and penned by mere mortals." But My set apart ones, people of My presence, will keep and honor My Word and will not turn away or compromise. They will unashamedly open their mouths and proclaim My word with bold confidence.

The manifestation of My grace will increase in this hour and will be weighty on those whose hearts are turned toward Me. I am at work within My people both to will and to do of My good pleasure (Phil. 2:13).

It is time to seek the Lord and to turn away from all forms of evil, no matter how subtle they might seem. Love Me and serve Me with all your hearts, minds, and strength. Seek My presence. Do not fear those who may want to take your life but nothing more—the one you must fear is God.

In this hour, weighty words will be given to My church. Respond. Prepare. Remember who you are—you are My bride. I am coming for My bride who is without spot, wrinkle, or blemish. I have called you. I have sent My Spirit to prepare you. Lean into Me. Follow Me. Only Me. Maranatha (the Lord has come; the Lord is coming).

It is time to return with our whole hearts to the Lord. It is time to cease hesitating between two opinions. If the Lord is God, worship Him, follow Him, love Him.

We are living in days like those Elijah lived in. God is looking for voices who will speak the truth in love with uncompromised devotion and conviction. Are you one who has not bowed your knee to Baal? If you have, turn back to God and receive forgiveness. If you have not, raise your voice. Be heard. Open your mouth; He will fill it.

ABOUT PATRICIA KING

Patricia King is a respected apostolic minister of the gospel, successful business owner, and an inventive entrepreneur. She is an accomplished itinerant speaker, author, television host, media producer, and ministry network overseer who has given her life fully to Jesus Christ and to His Kingdom's advancement in the earth. She is the founder of Patricia King Ministries and co-founder of XPmedia.com.

Chapter 10

PACESETTERS, ARISE!

Sarah Cheesman

On Saturday, October 12, Kenyan athlete Eliud Kipchoge became the first man to run a marathon in under two hours. This is believed to be as significant as when Roger Barrister broke the four-minute mile. Listening to the commentators I heard one say, "I never thought I'd see this in my lifetime."

His average pace was a time of 2 minutes and 50 seconds per kilometer. That's the equivalent of 68 seconds per 400 meters or better still 17 seconds per 100 meters—for two hours.

He ran the perfect race on a course specifically marked out for him around a park in Vienna, Austria. At sea level, the city is set in perfect running conditions. Combined with immense preparation and a team of pacesetters replicating race-like conditions, the course was purpose-built for his success.

As I watched the last 30 minutes of the race, the kilometers passed by ever so quickly and it became clear that he would absolutely break the two-hour time barrier.

There were so many beautiful moments that were captured throughout and at the end of the race. I want to tell you about my favorite. It's not when Eliud crossed the finish line; it's not when they presented him with a trophy and the official time; it's not even when he embraced his wife at the end of the race. It's the moment when with 500 meters to go and the end in sight, his pacesetters peeled back from around him and began to cheer. They began to celebrate him and champion him until he crossed the finish line.

Tears filled my eyes in that moment and I heard the Holy Spirit whisper, "That's what family does." Moving into 2020, I sense this is what He is calling the Body of Christ into in this season.

Each of the men who ran with Kipchoge are elite, professional athletes and champions in their own right. They represent many countries and compete in a variety of running distances. However, in humility they laid down competition and comparison and gave themselves to seeing someone else succeed. They had to run just as fast, they had to break the headwind, and they had to train and know where to be when. But it's not their names that are beside the record; it's Kipchoge's. And they celebrated that they had the opportunity to not only be there, but to play a part in history. They gave their best to him so he could reach a goal and achieve a dream—more than that, so he could break through, which will enable others to do so as well.

I heard the Holy Spirit say, "I am calling My Body to set pace for one another in this season. I've prepared the course and now it's time for you, in humility, to prefer one another above yourself and do all you can to come alongside others to bring them success. This new era will be marked by My Body giving herself to one another in love to see the greatest victories in the earth and dreams coming to pass! Don't run for yourself—join the race and run for someone else!"

He then revealed to me that pacesetters do three things:

- They set the course
- They protect the runner
- They set the pace

THEY SET THE COURSE

Kipchoge's pacesetters had a race marked out for them to follow and that enabled him to stay the course. They ran the most efficient course so all he had to do was to continue to move ahead. Like mothers and fathers would, they guided him along the path he should take.

I was reminded of 1 Timothy 1:18: "*This charge I entrust to you, Timothy, my child, in accordance with the prophecies previously made about you, that by them you may wage the good warfare.*" In this verse Paul is actually reminding Timothy to keep his eyes on where he's going, to remember the words spoken over him. He is encouraging him to pursue them wholeheartedly. By reminding him about the truth of who he was called to be, Paul was marking out the path for him.

I heard the Father say, "I am calling you to call out the gold in others in this season. Speak life and use your words to set the course in which they should run."

They Protect

In Kipchoge's race, the pacesetters made an arrow formation in front of him and two flanked him at the back. This was to protect him from the wind and outdoor elements. Essentially, they were creating a human shield.

I heard the Holy Spirit say, "It's time to raise the shield of faith for one another. Commit to praying for one another and go to war for the destiny of those you're called to run with."

Notice the pacesetters covered his back as well. I sense the Father is setting a standard in the Church again where we'll be people who refuse to speak ill of one another or produce gossip and slander.

Love one another with brotherly affection. Outdo one another in showing honor (Romans 12:10).

It's time to stop shooting arrows into the backs of others. Instead, we have an opportunity to make it our mission to cover and protect them. In this new era, we're required to operate differently if we desire to see different results. We must refuse to compromise the standard of righteousness in how we treat one another; especially our leaders.

When running together, pacesetters break the wind barrier enabling the runner to move into the ease of the slipstream. I heard the Spirit say, "There are those whom I am calling you to break-through for in this season so they can enjoy the ease of the race. This looks like laying down your life for your friends for kingdom purpose. The victory that I will give you is so much bigger than just the individual I would have you run with. As each one takes their place in the formation, corporately you will become a family of overcomes and victorious ones who win battles for the Kingdom and advance in the earth."

THEY SET THE PACE

There is a consistency required to break barriers of destiny. Upon beginning the race, Kipchoge's goal was to complete the course in one hour, 59 minutes and 50 seconds. That's just 10 seconds shy of two hours. When it comes to kilometer split times, across 42 kilometers, that does not leave a lot of margin for error.

In the race the pacesetters were able to correct the average speed when required in order to maintain the pace needed to run sub-two hours. I heard the Spirit say, "By setting the pace for others you enable them to endure the changes of life, and in the times that are difficult you can help them to remain steadfast and secure. Then they are able to be like the wise man who built his house upon the rock" (see Matt. 7:24-27).

Kipchoge not only beat two hours, he ran a time of one hour, 59 minutes and 40.2 seconds. That's approximately 10 seconds quicker than his goal. Kipchoge's pacesetters didn't let the kilometers that were off pace dictate the overall outcome. The Lord reminded me of Philippians 3:13-14: *"One thing I do: forgetting what lies behind and straining forward to what lies ahead, I press on toward the goal for the prize of the upward call of God in Christ Jesus."*

Coming alongside and laying down our lives for our friends means overlooking the inconsistencies of pace and going the distance, seeing the race through, and ensuring victory for those with whom we run!

Humility and Vulnerability

I also sensed the encouragement of the Holy Spirit in this season to become vulnerable with one another. Kipchoge is the most decorated and celebrated long-distance runner—he's the current Olympic champion and world record holder. He's believed to be the greatest long-distance runner ever, and yet he recognized he couldn't run alone!

In all his ability and proof to back it up, in humility, he acknowledged he needed the help of others to make it across the line in time. I hear the Spirit's encouragement, "Don't run in isolation." It doesn't matter how naturally gifted you are, Kipchoge displayed vulnerability in saying, "I can't do this alone; I need you to run with me."

God is setting us up for success in this era, but for you to fulfill all He has for you in the earth it will require a team of people around you to champion you. This brings an end to all jealousy and comparison. He is calling His Body to recognize the gift of the different parts and not to try to compete or be like the other but celebrate what they have to contribute and, more than that, run so the other can be all they were created to be.

An Invitation

I sense this is an invitation from the Holy Spirit looking for our response. Moving into 2020, I encourage you to ask the Holy Spirit the following:

- Who am I called to set pace for in this season?
- Who am I called to lay my life down for to see them advance?

- Who am I going to break the headwind for so they don't have to?

- Who am I meant to come alongside to champion today?

You may find you are called to different ones in different seasons. Kipchoge's team had different combinations of different runners at different times. But there was always a team consistently there who moved seamlessly in and out of the race. On the other hand, there may be some whom you're called to go the entire distance with as well and that is equally as valuable. We can't win without one another. As family this is what we do.

> *Let us also lay aside every weight, and sin which clings so closely, and let us run with endurance the race that is set before us, looking to Jesus, the founder and perfecter of our faith* (Hebrews 12:1-2).

Jesus is the ultimate pacesetter—let's live like Him and lay our lives down for our friends as we run for them. By doing so I believe it will usher us into the fullness of this new era, positioning us for success as we esteem others above ourselves. The personal victory of individuals will become a corporate breakthrough for the Body to enter into.

> *Let love be the beautiful prize for which you run* (1 Corinthians 13:13 TPT).

> *But the fruit produced by the Holy Spirit within you is divine love in all its varied expressions: joy that overflows, peace that subdues, patience that endures, kindness in action, a life full of virtue, faith that prevails,*

gentleness of heart, and strength of spirit. Never set the law above these qualities, for they are meant to be limit-less (Galatians 5:22-23 TPT).

This is the consistency of spirit in which we are called to run!

ABOUT SARAH CHEESMAN

Sarah Cheesman loves the fellowship of the Holy Spirit and believes that hearing the voice of God is natural for every believer and, indeed, their birthright! She carries a heart for societal transformation and encourages the Church to give their hearts in prayer to see battles won in the heavenlies and to receive strategies that are effective for change in the earth.

She sits on the Australian Prophetic Council, leads their up-and-coming prophets, and is a prophetic voice to the Glory City Network. Additionally, she teaches weekly at The Academy, facilitates the School of the Prophets at Glory City Church, and leads their prophetic community. She also hosts her own podcast, The Happy Prophet Podcast.

Sarah and her husband Jesse live in Brisbane, Australia and have two small children—Lucy and Harry.

Chapter 11

2020: The Year of Extravagant Asking

Mario Murillo

On August 11, 1927, Smith Wigglesworth stood in Angelus Temple to preach on the subject of preparing for the Second Coming of Christ. He told the audience that liquid fire was consuming him. Little did he realize the prophetic word that he was delivering was for you and I—and is for this very hour in which we live. The accuracy of his words pertaining to the present church is stunning.

I believe that he was seeing a cataclysmic event—an event that will reach its apex in 2020. After many deceptions, distractions, and setbacks, God's core people will emerge in great power. The one thing that will mark them in 2020 is *extravagant asking*.

Smith made this opening statement:

> But there will be things that will happen prior to His coming that we shall know. You can tell. I am like one this morning that is moving with a liquid, holy, indispensable, real fire in my bosom, and I know it is burning and (yet) the body is not consumed. It is real fire from heaven that is making my utterances come to you to (assure you) that He is coming. He is on the way. God is going to help me tell you why you will know. You that have the breath of the Spirit, there is something now moving as I speak. As I speak, this breath of mighty, quickening, moving, changing, desirable power is making you know; and it is this alone that is making you know that you will be ready.

1. There must be special preparation for the return of Christ and at least half of all believers will be totally unprepared.

We have to see that these days have to come before the Lord can come. There has to be a falling away.

I want to speak to you very exactly. All the people who are pressing into and getting ready for this glorious attained place where they shall not be found naked, where they shall be blameless, where they shall be immovable, where they shall be purified by the power of the Word of God, have within them a consciousness of the very presence of God within, changing their very nature and preparing them for a greater thing, and causing them to be ready for translation.

This is the day of purifying. This is the day of holiness. This is the day of separation. This is the day of waking. O God, let us wake today! Let the inner spirit wake into consciousness that God is calling us.

There are in the world two classes of believers. There are believers who are disobedient, or I ought to say there are children who are saved by the power of God who are disobedient children. And there are children who are just the same, saved by the power of God, who all the time are longing to be more obedient.

And we heard the word come rushing through, all over: "new theology" that damnable, devilish, evil power that lived in some of these disobedient children, which in these last days opened the door to the next thing.

2. *There will be many Christians who believe that they can do whatever they want and God will look the other way.*

People are tremendously afraid of this position because they have heard so much on this line: "Oh, you know you are the elect of God! You are sure to be all right." There have been in England great churches which were laid out upon these things. I thank God that they are all withered. You will find if you go to England those strong people that used to hold all these things are almost withered out. Why? Because they went on to say whatever you did, if you were elect, you were right, and that is wrong.

The elect of God are those who are pressing forward.

3. It will be common for preachers to deny the existence of hell. Denying hell prepares the way for antichrist.

What? No hell? The devil has always said that. What does Christian Science say? "No hell, no devil." They are ready for him. The devil has always said, "(There is) no hell, no evil." And these people are preparing, and they do not know it, for the Man of Sin.

4. It is offensive to talk about the Blood of Christ.

When I spoke about the blood and when I spoke about this infernal thing, the whole place was upset. You be careful when anybody comes to you with a sugar-coated pill or with a slimy tongue. They are always of the devil. The Spirit of the Lord will always deal with Truth. These people never deal with Truth. They always cover up the Truth.

Do you believe it? Who can do it? *The blood can do it!* The blood, the blood, oh the blood! The blood of the Lamb! The blood of Jesus can do it. Spotless, clean, preserved for God.

Give the devil the biggest chase of his life and say these words, "The blood of Jesus Christ, God's Son, cleanses us from all unrighteousness!"

5. People believe that certain preachers are of God simply because of their crowds and their buildings.

A person said to me, "You see, the Christian Scientists must be right—look at the beautiful buildings. Look at all the people following them."

Yes, everybody can belong to it. You can go to any brother you like, you can go to any theater you like, you can go to any race course you like, you can be mixed up with the rest of the people in your life and still be a Christian Scientist. You can have the devil right and left and anywhere, and still belong to Christian Science.

6. As churches turn away from the Holy Spirit, many believers go to false teachers.

The secret of many people going into Christian Science is a barren church that had not the Holy Ghost. Christian Science exists because the churches have a barren place and because they haven't the Holy Ghost. There would be no room for Christian Science if the churches were filled with the Holy Ghost.

7. The last days are a time for the true people of God to engage in extravagant asking.

Up to this present time the Lord's word is for us, "Hitherto ye have asked nothing." Surely you people that have been asking great things from God for a long time would be amazed if you entered into it with clear knowledge that it is the Master, it is Jesus, who has such knowledge of the mightiness of the power of the Father, of the joint union with Him, that nothing is impossible for you to ask. Surely it is He only Who could say "Hitherto you have asked nothing."

So God means me to press you another step forward. Begin to believe in *extravagant asking*, believing that God is pleased when you ask large things.

I believe that his last point is the main thing for us to take away about 2020. Many believers are sick of "church incorporated." They know there has to be more than the shallow "entertainment centers" that churches have become. They know we have lost our culture.

They believe they are to be separated and fitted for a great act of God. 2020 is the do-or-die year of the American church. We will either be restored or we will be removed.

God is warring to restore us and lead us into untold greatness. That is why 2020 is the year of *extravagant asking*. It is the year to ask for big things—things that will boggle the mind. Things we assumed were out of our reach.

The *extravagant asking* must be expressed in several kinds of requests. We must ask for profound purity and intimacy with God. We are about to be trusted with resources that should only be in the hands of those with a clean heart.

We must not be outside technology lamenting its influence, we must be led into it—into the very thick of it. We must bring it "captive to the obedience of Christ."

We must ask for inventions. We must also understand that not everyone belongs behind a pulpit. Some make history in other ways. Inventions, solutions, and many breakthroughs are waiting to be imparted.

We must be prophetic in a way that matters. This towering gift must not be misspent in safe meetings and squandered on mutual flattery. The prophetic speaks truth to power. It is the spirit of Elijah pointing the finger of God at wickedness and killing it at the root.

Prophets must make enemies—the right kind of enemies—the enemies of God. The Left has wholly given itself over to pagan worship, witchcraft, and hatred of Judeo-Christian values. Prophets are not supposed to hide in the church hoping to be invited to the right conferences to keep their book sales up. They are supposed to bring down the false prophets of Baal, which in our case are the secular progressives.

We must ask for resources. It is not enough to recite the words, "The wealth of the wicked is laid up for the just." We must have a plan, a discipline, and a perseverance to enforce that promise.

Our current weakness, lack, and failure is summed up in these simple words: "You have not because you ask not."

2020 is the year of *extravagant asking* because our need is extravagant, our enemy is extravagant, and the threat is extravagant. Nothing defines you more than what you ask for in prayer. Remember, Jesus said, *"all things for which you pray and ask, believe that you have received them, and they will be granted you"* (Mark 11:24 NASB).

ABOUT MARIO MURILLO

Mario Murillo rose from poverty in the Mission District of San Francisco. After being revolutionized by Christ, he felt a call to the riot-torn University of California at Berkeley. He was rejected until a desperate prayer season resulted in supernatural power. It began with preaching that was different than students had ever heard. Then the students began to report healings in the Name of Jesus. A four-day crusade in San Jose, California lasting six months with over 250,000 people birthed an international ministry that is reaching millions!

Chapter 12

The Decade of Declaration and Acceleration

Katherine Ruonala

2020! What an exciting time to be alive! We have just entered a new decade and a whole new era for the Body of Christ. As we enter this new decade, there is an excitement in my spirit for what I see as a window of favor and opportunity for the gospel. I keep hearing the song "I can see clearly now," and I believe as we enter in 2020 God is inviting us into clear, 20/20 vision so that we see, believe, and decree with clarity and faith (see Mark 11:23). Having watched as the Body of Christ has been increasingly learning how to see and hear prophetically from the Lord, I believe there is a maturing of the Bride as she comes into a new understanding of her authority to speak and declare what she is seeing and hearing, with a holy boldness birthed out of a holy conviction of who she is in Christ. There is a Holy Spirit invitation into awakening and it is an invitation that requires a response.

DECADE OF PROPHETIC DECLARATION 5780

The Hebrew letter for the number 80 is פ —pronounced *peh*. *Peh* is also the Hebrew word for mouth, and so many prophets are declaring this new decade a decade of declaring the will of the Lord.

Now as believers, we should be aware of the power of our words. But in this new era, the Holy Spirit is awakening believers out of their slumber to begin to understand the greatness of the power we have and the urgency there is to exercise that power to partner with God in His plans and purposes for His name's sake. Proverbs tells us:

> *A man's stomach shall be satisfied from the fruit of his mouth; from the produce of his lips he shall be filled. Death and life are in the power of the tongue, and those who love it will eat its fruit* (Proverbs 18:20-21 NKJV).

For example, Joshua spoke to the sun and told it to stand still (see Josh. 10:12-14), being fully convinced that it was the will of God for Israel to entirely defeat its enemy. Elijah declared that there would be no dew or rain (see 1 Kings 17:1). Jesus modeled for us how to hear from the Father and then speak what He is saying (see John 12:49-50) and to calm storms and wither a fig tree by the power of His words (see Mark 4:39-41; 11:20-21). And then, as we have seen, Jesus taught His disciples to speak to mountains and expect them to move (see Mark 11:22-24). He gave His followers the keys to the Kingdom and the power to bind and loose, all of which involves words of faith and authority. By creating us in His image, the God who created the world with His words gave us the same power.

> *Assuredly, I say to you, whoever says to this mountain, "Be removed and be cast into the sea," and does not doubt in his heart, but believes that those things he says will be done, he will have whatever he says. Therefore I say to you, whatever things you ask when you pray, believe that you receive them, and you will have them* (Mark 11:23-24).

As people who have been created in the image of God, we are made in the image of the one who created the world with His words. God calls those things that do not exist as though they did (see Rom. 4:17). In the same way, 2020 will be a year that people awaken again to the importance of creating with their words.

Out of the abundance of the heart, the mouth speaks (see Matt. 12:34). This is part of your transition from the pattern of the world and renewing your mind in truth. It will become more natural as you go on, but begin by being very intentional to speak life over your own life, your spouse, your children, your extended family members, your friends, co-workers, acquaintances, and every sphere of influence you have. Instead of talking about how difficult or dark or oppressing some obligation or relationship might be, talk about how you are the fragrance of Christ and His Spirit goes with you into every corner of your world to bring light and life into it. Declare that the Lord is your strength and with Him there's nothing you can't do. Declare that your home or your workplace is getting brighter and brighter, filled more and more with the glory of God. Jesus is in you, and wherever you go He is being released there through your words—if you have conditioned yourself to speak life.

So ask yourself: what are you creating with your words? As I mentioned, I've been partnering with God to create with my tongue for most of the last two decades, and I am seeing things unfold now that I spoke years ago. It's really remarkable. We are called in the Holy Spirit to see and to say, and then we will experience what we've seen and said. He wants us to go ahead and get happy about already having received the miracles and blessings we do not yet see with our natural eyes. Why? Because that makes us a lot like Him—the God who calls things that are not as though they are, who named Abraham the father of many nations before he had even had a son. He has not changed. He invites us to enter into what He did in the pages of Scripture and what He is still doing in many lives now. He wants us to declare creatively what He is inviting us into, to create with our words, and to speak life.

Awake, Awake!

Awake, awake! Put on your strength, O Zion (Isaiah 52:1).

The word of God and prophetic promises are not necessarily inevitabilities but invitations requiring our response. The Holy Spirit is awakening His Bride to recognize the times and seasons, and I believe a fresh sense of urgency to bring the hope of Christ to the world is stirring the Body of Christ to action. *The fields are white unto harvest!* (See John 4:35.) God is awakening an evangelistic movement that will take full advantage of the season of favor we have been given. In speaking to a farmer friend recently, he explained to me that when grain is ready for harvest, the fields are golden and harvesting begins in earnest. The next stage after golden is white, but a white harvest indicates that the grain is overripe and that is when you really have to harvest with all your focus and energy. A white harvest is easier to bring in, because the grain literally falls into your hand, but there is a great urgency to bring the harvest in once the fields turn white, because adverse winds could blow the grain away before it is brought in. But there is also a great urgency to hurry and harvest when the fields are white, as the next stage after white is when the fields turn black, and then it is too late to harvest any more. I believe we have an unprecedented opportunity to bring a mass harvest of souls right now, as we have a window of favor and opportunity. As my farmer friend would say, we must "make hay while the sun shines!"

The fields are ripe but the laborers are few (see Luke 10:2). Pray to the Lord of the harvest to send forth the laborers into the harvest field. The Lord is sending us; we must listen and ask His help to use each one of us to bring in the lost in this season.

Divine Acceleration, Refined Focus

2020 is also a time of supernatural acceleration. Everything is being accelerated, knowledge is increasing, but both the wheat and the tares will grow at an accelerated rate in this season. Pray for discernment and wisdom and be very careful what you focus on in this season. We need to be aware that a wave of acceleration is coming and it will move forward to what you are focused on. Be careful to mind your own business, walk in love and the fear of the Lord, and fix your eyes on what has eternal importance in this season.

Awake to Righteousness

There is a fresh awakening blowing on the hearts of believers in this era and people are waking up to the simplicity of justification by faith as the only means to walk in holiness. This awakening is causing people to realize that wisdom is justified by her actions and must be applied if it is to have any benefit. It is a call to true holiness, but it is being made clear that this can only be achieved by applying what we know about righteousness to our everyday choices.

"If our heart does not condemn us, we have confidence toward God" and can know we will have what we ask of Him, writes John in one of his letters. And if our heart does condemn us? *"God is greater than our heart"* (1 John 3:20-22).

When we have put our faith in Jesus, we believe we have been crucified with Him, buried with Him, and raised up with Him. We are new creations. *"As He is, so are we in this world"* (1 John 4:17), and we are the righteousness of God in Christ (see 2 Cor. 5:21). Because God is perfect light and can have no fellowship with darkness and sin, He did everything necessary to make us completely clean. We have to have faith that we are forgiven so that we can walk in our identity as saints. We can fully believe that He is giving His Son a Bride that is compatible, equally yoked, and perfectly suited for His supernatural, incorruptible nature. We have been set free from fear, guilt, shame, condemnation, worry, anxiety, heaviness, sickness, and every other work of the evil one. If we have repented of our sin and put our faith in the Savior, we have been made as righteous as God and can walk in His power. Knowing this we must then recognize and put on our new "super powers" and live lives that bring Christ glory.

Like the hearer of the Word in James 1, so many Christians have walked away from the mirror and forgotten what they look like. Jesus as He is portrayed in Scripture is our true image—we can have His mind, hear His voice, and do His works in the same power He demonstrated. We can be as righteous as He is, and in fact, by

His sacrifice on our behalf, we already are and have power to walk as such. As believers, we have been transferred from the kingdom of darkness into the Kingdom of light. We are no longer sinners. Light can't have fellowship with darkness, so He has made us as righteous as He is so we can be joined to Him. He has taken away every trace of our iniquity, our crookedness. He gives us His righteousness, His holiness, His nature. Then we have the responsibility and the power to put this righteousness to work in our lives, walking out righteousness by faith, putting into practice what has been given to us through salvation.

That's our invitation, and God is asking us to walk in it supernaturally—not by our own efforts, but by putting Him on by faith and wearing Him, being filled with Him, and expressing Him wherever we go. It's an astonishing, glorious, and much needed truth today as we enter this season of acceleration.

Convergence and Promises Fulfilled

2020 is also a time of divine convergence, when many will find themselves walking in the things they have long dreamed of. But it is not time to slow down; instead, we need to start swimming to catch the wave of acceleration that is coming so that we can be propelled forward into our destinies.

We also need to remain vigilant to prioritize our personal times with the Lord. With so much to do, and with so many good things calling for our time, time spent alone in the secret place will become more important than ever. We need Him! The Holy Spirit is our ever-present help in times of need and we need a revelation that our time of need is all the time—on the mountains and in the valleys.

Jesus People

It has long been prophesied that there is a new Jesus People movement coming and we have seen this beginning, particularly in Australia. Church, get ready—we need to be ready to receive with joy these brand-new young converts and love them and listen to them without judgement, showing them the way of Christ in the context of true family.

Divine Exchange

> *Instead of your [former] shame you shall have a twofold recompense; instead of dishonor and reproach [your people] shall rejoice in their portion. Therefore in their land they shall possess double [what they had forfeited]; everlasting joy shall be theirs* (Isaiah 61:7 AMPC).

God is waiting to awaken us to the understanding of the divine exchange table, where He gives beauty for ashes. As we awaken to the realities of life as a believer, I believe the Holy Spirit is breathing fresh understanding on the application and response we have to the Word of God. We can bring our pain, shame, and disgrace and exchange it in faith for double recompense.

> *Return to the stronghold, you prisoners of hope. Even today I declare that I will restore double to you* (Zechariah 9:12 NKJV).

The number 20 can be a symbol of redemption, as well a symbol of completion and perfection. I believe this year we must awaken to the importance of exchanging our beauty for ashes and to take those things like pain, loss, and shame, which are foreign currency in the Kingdom, and bring them to the divine exchange table. Just like we exchange foreign currency, we need to activate faith to exchange those things that we have been through. The invitation is, "Double for your trouble!"

CONCLUSION

Finally, in this time of acceleration we need to make a choice to keep preaching the message of the simplicity of Christ and Him crucified as our main objective. Statistics tell us that 41,000 people a day die without hearing and having an opportunity to respond to the gospel. There is an urgency to take the message of Jesus to a lost world, and there are no good excuses for any of us to stand on the sidelines. There is so much opportunity to see Christ lifted up in our lives, and we must be willing to recognize the time and start swimming to catch the wave that is coming.

ABOUT KATHERINE RUONALA

Katherine Ruonala carries a strong prophetic and miracle anointing with many being instantly healed in her meetings. Reaching across denominational walls, her ministry is also used to spread the fires of revival and ignite a fresh passion in the hearts of believers to go deeper in their relationship with God. Katherine is a wife, mother, accomplished author and founder of Glory City Church in Brisbane.

Chapter 13

CIVIL WAR, REVOLUTIONARY WAR, HEAVEN'S PERSPECTIVE ON AMERICA, AND THE RELEASE OF CHAMPIONS

Rick Joyner

In December of 2018, I had a prophetic dream in which I was shown America's history from Heaven's perspective. It was very different from any history I had read. For example, Heaven did not consider America as having won the Revolutionary War. They did not see this as a war to free ourselves from British rule to establish a nation where everyone was truly considered equal, as stated in the Declaration of Independence. If this had been accomplished, there would have been no reason for the Civil War because there could not have been slavery or even discrimination.

The difference between Heaven's perspective of American history and our earthly perspective was striking in other captivating ways. However, I felt compelled to go see Heaven's perspective of our most recent history, where we are now. Instead of seeing unfolding events, I saw the following in brilliant fiery letters: "The Second American Revolutionary/Civil War is inevitable, it is right, and it will be successful."

Because of what I had seen of Heaven's perspective on our history, I understood why this was inevitable and some of why it was right. However, the dream ended while I was trying to see what "successful" meant from Heaven's perspective.

This dream was one of the most extraordinary I have ever had, and there was far more to it than can be covered in a short chapter. What I am sharing here is crucial for now.

This dream began with great champions receiving assignments by an angel to seek and destroy certain spiritual strongholds. The angel emphasized that these strongholds should not just be defeated or driven away but destroyed. I was reminded of how Joshua was told to utterly destroy the enemies of Israel or they would come back as stumbling blocks to Israel. There was a fierceness in this angel that was conveyed to these champions.

As these champions moved out to their task, others gathered to each one to help. This is beginning to happen now and will be one of the important developments unfolding in 2020. This will begin waking up Christians who have been inactive or dormant in congregations that are not really engaged in the battles of our times.

These champions, who are skilled in spiritual warfare and have authority from the Lord to attack these enemies, will win victories that will inspire many others to leave the sleeping congregations. They will inspire them to gather where real training and deployment is happening. The Christian leaders of the future church will be these warrior champions who are fighting the good fight.

In the dream, the champions sent out to destroy strongholds were told that these enemies would be found in trees. Trees are the biggest and strongest of all plants, and their strength is determined by the health of their roots. The enemies we are about to engage have deep and strong roots. We must not just flail at the branches, but rather put the axe to the roots of these trees.

Ineffective spiritual warfare, led by the immature or the shallow, has ultimately strengthened the enemy. This was sometimes done by driving out the enemy but failing to occupy the territory vacated. As Jesus explained, when a demon is cast out, it always tries to return. If it finds its former habitation unoccupied, it will bring back seven more, even worse than itself. This is true of territorial powers as well.

We must not continue to waste our energy and resources fighting battles until we are also ready to occupy and hold the ground taken. There will always be a counterattack, and the wise do not waste time celebrating or promoting their victories. Rather, they are preparing for the battles to come. In the dream, the champions about to be sent out were strong because of their depth—they were mature and deep in their understanding because they knew the Holy Spirit who searches the depths, even the depths of God.

No one who really knows and follows the Holy Spirit will be shallow. One way we can discern the future leaders is by their depth. We must have strong and deep roots to confront the deep and strong enemies we're facing.

This leads to another prophetic dream I had over ten years ago that is connected to the one above and will also begin to unfold now. In that dream, I saw many fathers from the back, but I knew who they were. I was told that if we would learn to honor our fathers, the Lord would bring revival to America within six months. By dishonoring fathers and fatherhood, one of the biggest gates of hell had been opened into our country. Gates of hell are the access points where the powers of hell enter our lives, the church, and the world.

As the apostle Paul explained in Ephesians 6, honoring our fathers and mothers is the only commandment with a promise attached. The promise is that it would go well with us, and we would have longevity on the earth. The intentional and systematic strategy of our enemy to have us dishonor our fathers and mothers is one reason why things are starting to go so badly for America.

A major way this dishonoring of our fathers is being done is through revisionist historians who have dishonored our national founding fathers. They have twisted and rewritten history to make some of the greatest men in history seem evil. Coupled with the assault on fatherhood and the assault on masculinity in general, this will destroy our Republic if not reversed. It will be reversed.

So how do we reverse this? We begin by obeying the commandment to honor our fathers and mothers. Although I was shown in my dream that we needed to focus on honoring the fathers, it's not possible to become a father without a mother being present. We also need to honor mothers and motherhood as it deserves. This is also a key to tearing down the stronghold of abortion.

Even so, it is fatherhood that has been under the greatest assault in our country and in many others, and so this needs our greatest attention. The exhortation in Malachi 4 is for restoring the hearts of the fathers to the children and the children to the fathers; there is no mention of mothers there.

There has no doubt been a "toxic masculinity" that has abused women and the weak throughout history. Even so, masculinity itself is not "toxic." Yet this is what is being taught in public schools and universities in order to corrupt the family, the basic social structure of society. True masculinity and true femininity are essential bulwarks against the deep darkness seeking to devour the world.

If we are going to go after the roots of what is attacking fatherhood and masculinity, then we must be deep and strong in what it means to be a father and a man. True men will have the utmost respect for true women. They will use their strength to help the weak, not abuse or use them for selfish means.

We must become resolute in teaching the young how to walk in the dignity and honor with which the sons and daughters of the King should conduct themselves. We must teach them how to treat the opposite sex with dignity and respect. We must intentionally teach men how to be men and women how to be women, according to the royal standards of the Lord.

The blurring of gender distinctions that God has made is a basic assault on the integrity of God and a basic strategy of the devil to cloak the world in a deep darkness that cannot be penetrated by the gospel. To say that God gave someone the body of one gender but the heart of the opposite gender is an affront to God. It implies that He did not know what He was doing but made such mistakes when He made us. This begins to erode our faith in Him in everything else.

Men and women who are in confusion about who they are will not be able to become who they were created to be unless the confusion is cleared up. Being who we are requires confidence in who we are, which requires clarity. This is how the light, or the truth, sets us free. The more light we can see, or the deeper the truth, the more confidence we have in it and the more we can accurately relate to it.

The spiritual champions about to be revealed will have clarity about who they are and what they are called to be. This is because they will have received their identity from God, not from the twisted, confused, and degrading philosophies of this fallen world. These future leaders are a new breed of leader and are God's freedom fighters. They will proclaim liberty throughout the land. This is basic to the gospel of the Kingdom that the Lord said must be preached throughout the world before the end of this age can come, and this we will soon begin to hear.

ABOUT RICK JOYNER

Rick Joyner has authored more than fifty books, including *The Final Quest Trilogy, There Were Two Trees in the Garden, The Path,* and *Army of the Dawn.* He is the Founder and Executive Director of MorningStar Ministries, a multi-faceted mission organization which includes Heritage International Ministries, MorningStar University, MorningStar Fellowship of Churches and Ministries, and CMM/MorningStar Missions—an umbrella organization serving over five hundred missionaries in the field and over ten thousand churches, schools, and ministries around the world. Rick and his wife, Julie, live in South Carolina and have five children: Anna, Aaryn, Amber, Ben, and Sam.

To receive more information about Rick Joyner or MorningStar Ministries, visit www.morningstarministries.org or check out his Facebook page at www.facebook.com/rickjoyner.morningstar/.

Chapter 14

2020–2029: The Era of the Nations

Arleen Westerhof

"Then He who sat on the throne said,
'Behold, I make all things new.'"
—Revelation 21:5 NKJV

2020 will be the year in which we enter the era of nations: *"And the nations of those who are saved shall walk in its light, and the kings of the earth bring their glory and honor into it. ...And they shall bring the glory and the honor of the nations into it"* (Rev. 21:24,26 NKJV).

Winds of change are blowing across the earth. These violent winds are blowing out the old era and ushering in the new. 2020 will mark the beginning of a decade of *unprecedented Kingdom advancement*, the *great harvest*, and the *age of righteous rule*.

Unprecedented Kingdom Advancement

In 2010 during a period in which our church was fasting and praying for 40 days, the Lord gave me a vision. In this vision I saw many believers standing at the border between the wilderness and the Promised Land. They were celebrating. They had made it through the wilderness and were ecstatic! As they worshiped and praised God, signs, wonders, and miracles were prevalent. They spent time admiring the Promised Land from the border and talking about how wonderful life would be now that they had arrived.

I was very surprised when, in the same vision, the Lord showed me the situation several years later. Memorials had been built to commemorate the great work of God in leading them through the wilderness, in addition to many churches. Some of these were thriving. They were, however, still on the border.

When He showed me the situation much later, I wept. An entire generation had lived and died on the border without ever entering the Promised land that still lay before them. Back then I wrote: "This will happen because many of us have not realized that breakthrough (revival) is not the victory. Breakthrough is a position from which we advance on toward the victory (reformation and transformation)."[1]

Fortunately, God has used the last decade to change our understanding of His Kingdom, and things are now in place for a new move of the Spirit unlike any that the world has ever seen. The Promised Land lies before us and the voice of the Lord is resounding, "Your battle is not against flesh and blood. It's against powers, principalities and spiritual forces of evil in the heavenly realms (see Eph. 6:12). Just like in the time of Gideon when the Midianites were everywhere at harvest time, so now those you battle against are everywhere! It's time to rise up and take the land! I promise to be with you as you move out at the sound of My voice. Now is the time of divine movement, so arise in the strength that you have and (re) take your nation!" (Judges 6:14).[2]

A Decade of Historic Battles

But the people who know their God shall be strong, and carry out great exploits (Daniel 11:32 NKJV).

Much ground has been lost and there are culture wars that need to be fought. I see a messenger angel crisscrossing the earth saying, "It's a brave new world! It's time for the brave to arise and take the land" (see Matt. 11:12). "Open your eyes," says the Lord. "I have gone up before you. Do not fear, for in spite of the opposition, I am with you! It's a season of heavenly visitations in which I will cause ordinary men and women to realize who they are in Me—mighty men and women of valor" (see Judg. 6:12).

These sons and daughters of God will rise up, shake off their fear, and confront the armies of darkness. It's time to engage in the battle and release the victory. The things that you have been through in the previous decade have prepared you for what God is calling us to do now, so arise and take the land. As He speaks, I see masses of people moving out and going where He leads.

The Great Harvest

And He said to them, "Go into all the world and preach the gospel to every creature. He who believes and is baptized will be saved; but he who does not believe will be condemned. And these signs will follow those who believe: In My name they will cast out demons; they will speak with new tongues; they will take up serpents; and if they drink anything deadly, it will by no means hurt them; they will lay hands on the sick, and they will recover" (Mark 16:15-18 NKJV).

2020 marks the start of a renewed missions mandate: the Gospel to every tribe, tongue, nation, and sphere of influence on the planet![3] Great doors are open in the Spirit for the preaching of the Gospel (see 1 Cor. 16:8-9; 2 Cor. 2:12). These doors will remain open during this new decade.

Some of the greatest harvest will come in from the nations that are most closed to the preaching of the gospel at this moment. "North Korea and the Middle East are Mine!" says the Lord. "Look to the 'silk road' that China is creating. It is My road and every nation that it runs through will be irrevocably changed by the preaching of the Gospel of Jesus Christ."

It is no longer just the Age of the Evangelist. This new decade will also be known as the Apostolic Age. Unusual signs and wonders will accompany the preaching of the gospel, and the church will return to her apostolic foundations to take the nations.

It's Time for the Born-Again Church

Another fruitful field for evangelism will be the church. Many know of Him but don't know Him. I hear the Holy Spirit saying, "It's time for the born-again church!" Churches based on purely intellectual Christianity will not be able to stand in this new decade.

A Shift in the Prayer Movement and Harvest

There's a shift occurring in the prayer movement as God pours out a spirit of boldness on His intercessors. This new era will see the proliferation of *contending houses of prayer*. Houses of prayer that wage war in the Spirit and know how to use their authority in the Courts of Heaven will be raised up to counter the increase in demonic attack against God's children. Strategic levels of intercession will be released to run together with evangelism to see the harvest of souls come in. The Spirit of the Lord is saying, "It's harvest time!"[4]

Baptizing Nations!

Through prophetic revelation I started an organization called the "Economic Summit." Our goal is to find and catalyze Holy Spirit-inspired solutions for global economic transformation. During our 2017 meeting in Cape Town, South Africa, one of the godliest women that I've ever met shocked us all when she said, "Will you Westerners please stop holding your evangelism campaigns in my nation!" As she spoke it was clear that she was visibly upset. She continued, "My nation in West Africa is 85 percent Christian. The vast majority of this 85 percent of people claim to be born again, but my nation is a mess! Our crime levels are off the charts. Corruption runs rampant. Our economy is in shambles, and people are starting to starve to death again in some of our rural areas." Then she said something that I will never forget: "We need less Christianity and more Christlikeness."

> And Jesus came and spoke to them, saying, "All authority has been given to Me in heaven and on earth. Go therefore and make disciples of all the nations, **baptizing them in the name of the Father and of the Son**

and of the Holy Spirit, teaching them to observe
all things that I have commanded you; and lo, I
am with you always, even to the end of the age." Amen
(Matthew 28:18-20 NKJV).

We're not just called to baptize individuals. We're called to baptize nations in the name of the Father, the Son, and the Holy Spirit. We do this by baptizing individuals *and* by bringing cultural transformation. Cultural transformation has eternal value:

> *The city [the New Jerusalem] had no need of the sun or*
> *of the moon to shine in it, for the glory of God illumi-*
> *nated it. The Lamb is its light. And the nations of those*
> *who are saved shall walk in its light, and* **the kings of**
> **the earth bring their glory and honor into it**" (Reve-
> lation 21:23-24 NKJV).

What is the glory of the nations? It is the best of culture that those nations have to offer. Jesus is worthy of nations. In this new era, winning people to Christ and equipping them to do the same, as well as transform culture, will once again become the core of Christian discipleship.

THE AGE OF RIGHTEOUS RULE

> *Behold, a king will reign in righteousness, and princes*
> *will rule with justice* (Isaiah 32:1).

There's a reign of righteousness that is shifting in the earth and it will manifest itself through political shifts across the globe as God replaces unrighteous leaders with righteous ones. We will, how-ever, have to battle to see this happen. Holy Spirit-led decrees and proclamations will bring about the breakthrough and cause a new civil order in government to be established. Many will change careers as God calls them into the civil arena and politics.

The Bible is clear. We are called to rule and to reign (see Gen. 1:26-28; Rom. 5:17).[5] Much of the Church has been uncomfortable with this idea because, since the Reformation, we have focused solely on our priestly calling as the Body of Christ. We have taught people how to pray, but we haven't taught them how to release justice. Priests counsel kings. Kings release justice (see Ps. 101:8).

"Righteousness and justice are the foundation of Your throne; mercy and truth go before Your face" (Ps. 89:14 NKJV). Releasing righteousness and justice is God's priority. In this new season, it will become our priority.

A New Level of Authority Attached to the Proclamation of the Prophetic Word

Last year I wrote: "At creation, God's Spirit hovered over the waters. Suddenly, the sound of His voice burst forth: 'Let there be light!' Then there was light. This season is about the power of the sound that God is calling us to release on the earth. As we issue supernaturally inspired decrees and call forth what we hear in the Spirit, God will release a new level of supernatural power, joined to the prophetic, so that the impossible (humanly speaking) becomes possible and manifests here on the earth."[6]

2020 will see a new generation of Elijah prophets raised up. These prophets will stand before kings and rulers and proclaim the word of the Lord. They will say, "At my word, this specific thing will happen so that you may know that there is a God in Heaven who presides over the affairs of men." God will back up the words of His prophets and will display Himself as El Shaddai through this new release of power through the prophetic that will cause nations to shift into their destinies and the timing of God.

This is the era in which God says: "Ask of Me and I *will* give you the nations!" (See Psalm 2:8.)

NOTES

1. Arleen Westerhof, "Advance from Breakthrough into Victory," December 8, 2011, http://www.elijahlist.com/words/display_word .html?ID=10524.

2. We (re)take our nations by prayer, proclaiming Holy Spirit-led decrees and engaging the seven mountains of culture.

3. Arleen Westerhof, *IMPACT: Prophesy and Change the World*, (Amsterdam, Netherlands: Arrowz USA in conjunction with Mandate Publishing, 2019), 142.

4. Arleen Westerhof, "'This Time Next Year...' is What I Hear the Spirit of the Lord Saying," Janauary 30, 2019, http://www.elijahlist .com/words/display_word.html?ID=21510.

5. In Genesis 1:26, God says, "Let them have dominion over the fish of the sea, over the birds of the air, and over the cattle, over all the earth and over every creeping thing that creeps on the earth." We have been given dominion over creation, but not over each other.

6. Westerhof, "This Time Next Year..." http://www.elijahlist.com/ words/display_word.html?ID=21510.

ABOUT ARLEEN WESTERHOF

Arleen Westerhof was born in Jamaica in the West Indies and grew up in Toronto, Canada. After completing her Ph.D. in Chemistry, she moved to the UK to work at the University of London before moving to Amsterdam to work as an expatriate for a large multinational corporation. 12 years later God called her into full-time ministry.

Arleen is the founder and facilitator of the Netherlands Prophetic Council. She is also the lead pastor, together with her husband Dick, of the God's Embassy Church in Amsterdam. Embassy started in the city centre close to the Red Light District and from the very beginning they and several of the members of the church have been involved in ministering to the prostitutes and other victims of human trafficking.

Arleen has a passion to help believers receive revelation aimed at advancing God's Kingdom in every one of the Seven Mountains of Influence. This was a major factor in prompting her to start the European Economic Summit, a semi-annual invitation-only Summit which aims to introduce new paradigms on finance and economy which are inspired by Christian tradition, faith and thought, and to present transformational businesses as new models for poverty alleviation and sustainable economies. Arleen is also the Chairperson of the European Evangelical Alliance's Economics Network.

Chapter 15

THE RUMBLE OF CULTURE-SHAKING REVIVAL AND AWAKENING

Gene Bailey

The year 2020 will bring many things to not only the Body of Christ and the church as a whole but to the nations as well. The word *revival* has become an overarching banner in Christian circles like never before. Of course, revival has been on the lips and in the hearts of many leaders in the church for decades. But not every church leader and congregation has a desire for an outpouring. So, what must change?

We have to re-dig the wells of revival of those who have gone before us just like Isaac did in Genesis 26:18, *"And Isaac digged again the wells of water, which they had digged in the days of Abraham his father; for the Philistines had stopped them after the death of Abraham"* (KJV).

What happens to a well that has been stopped up? Dirt has been thrown back in on top of the clean water until we have dirty water, or we do not see any water at all. And that is what we have right now in much of Christianity—stopped up wells and dirty water. The wells full of the dirty water of compromise have to be cleaned out. We need an old-fashioned return to holiness. I am not referring to a fleshly holiness dependent on our works either. We have seen that has no power. The only way for this to happen is a return to right relationship with God with a personal intimacy with Him. But, in the midst of all this, I do see hope and a difference growing in the Body.

The difference now is revival is on the lips and in the prayers of many everyday men and women from every demographic and every age group. That is truly exciting and an earmark of the spiritual temperature within the church. Church as we knew it is beginning to change.

History shows that when a hunger for God crosses generations like it is today, revival soon follows. The "millennials" (those born between 1981 to 1996) for a large part have been dismissed as not contributing significantly to the church. They have been described as not impacting the church either financially or spiritually. But that is changing. Already, we see a great shift in this generation toward intimacy with God and a yielding to the Holy Spirit. It reminds me of the Jesus movement during the 1960s through the 1970s.

The most exciting shift I am hearing is from the statesmen of the faith speaking of a "merging of the streams." Past movements seemed to only congregate around their denomination or segment of church culture. We are seeing older generations acknowledging the younger generations' callings and also their methods as well. Walking on stage in a t-shirt and jeans does not automatically make you a part of a new generation or a Jesus culture. A quantum shift in our normal church philosophy is evidenced by seeing an older generation in a suit and tie arm in arm with a t-shirt and jeans group worshiping God together from the platform.

Simplicity will be an earmark in this new awakening. In the Great Awakening the key issue was that salvation was for everyone. George Whitefield, John Wesley, and Jonathan Edwards led this culture-changing return to God.

Of course, we do indeed "study to show ourselves approved" as directed in 2 Timothy 2:15 TPT:

> *Always be eager to present yourself before God as a perfect and mature minister, without shame, as one who correctly explains the Word of Truth.*

There is more! I am referring to the life-changing simplicity of the gospel that reaches every social and economic level of mankind. Along with the simplicity of the gospel, there must be a return to pure unadulterated worship. I am encouraged to see it is already happening across the nations. I believe what we are already beginning to see in worship is perhaps one of the most important factors in this 2020 revival. I am not referring to smoke and skinny jeans and the cool factor here. I am seeing a real move of God happening right before my eyes.

What does that look like? Is it somber music and dimly lit auditoriums? Not necessarily. While we can certainly worship in that environment and see a move of God there, that does not mean that is the *only* way to see a move of God. In fact, that has been a cheap substitute for the fellowship connection with Holy Spirit in many churches in the last decades.

It has got to be the inside and the outside expression of worship. We cannot have just one-sided worship. Jesus said in Matthew 15:8-9:

> *This people honors me with their lips, but their heart is far from me; in vain do they worship me.*

Until we really put aside our own ideas about all the elements of worship, our experience there will amount to absolutely nothing. Also, Jesus said to us in John 4:23-24:

> *But the hour is coming, and is now here, when the true worshipers will worship the Father in spirit and truth, for the Father is seeking such people to worship him. God is spirit, and those who worship him must worship in spirit and truth.*

It is not about us or how we look; it truly is about who He is.

This worship, coupled with a desire to become more in love with who God really is and what Jesus did for us, will lead to a deeper and more intense fellowship with Him. Desire does not mean we must first attain a certain level of Christian faith in order to see God move.

Yes, we need revival. But not revival as some two-week event. We all desire more than that. Revival is indeed a refreshing and a return to God. What comes next is what we need more than the trappings of what most of us remember when we say the word *revival*. True revival leads to an *awakening*. An awakening will change the *culture*.

The more I search through history, the more I find all revivals had one common denominator. It is not difficult to see, but when mentioned it evokes pain in a lot of Christian faces. I used to be one of those faces! I am talking about prayer. Prayer must be the foundation to see a change in our own lives, much less ignite a revival. That is precisely what we need. Prayer.

To better understand this, the word *prayer* needs to be replaced with the words *intimacy with God*. We have a tendency to think of prayer as a laborious act of pleading with God, weeping, groaning, and lying prostrate on the floor for hours. While it can certainly be that, that is not the sum total of what God is desiring. He is asking for *us*. We must give Him one hundred percent of ourselves with no closed off rooms in our heart. To be intimate with God is to be fully immersed with Him to the point that we allow Jesus to be more evident than anything else.

All we have to do is look at the world around us to see the need for an awakening. In government, politics, our public schools, and even our churches. Yes, we need a return to God.

Recently, God really arrested me about something. Without realizing it, many of us have slowly departed from the simple truth of the gospel. Again, it is simplicity. It is not that we have purposely denied the salvation message; it is just that we do not preach it much anymore. Hard to believe isn't it?

> *Son of man, I have made you a watchman for the people of Israel; so hear the word I speak and give them warning from me. When I say to a wicked person, "You will surely die," and you do not warn them or speak out*

to dissuade them from their evil ways in order to save their life, that wicked person will die for their sin, and I will hold you accountable for their blood. But if you do warn the wicked person and they do not turn from their wickedness or from their evil ways, they will die for their sin; but you will have saved yourself.

Again, when a righteous person turns from their righteousness and does evil, and I put a stumbling block before them, they will die. Since you did not warn them, they will die for their sin. The righteous things that person did will not be remembered, and I will hold you accountable for their blood. But if you do warn the righteous person not to sin and they do not sin, they will surely live because they took warning, and you will have saved yourself (Ezekiel 3:17-21 NIV).

There is no better example of a revival than when someone gives their heart to God. Once dead in sin, now alive in Christ! We must pick up the salvation message again and preach it wherever we go. I do not want anyone's blood on my hands because I did not share the gospel with them. I am sure you do not want that either!

William Booth, founder of the Salvation Army, said, "I'm not waiting on a move of God, I *am* a move of God." At first look this statement sounds a bit arrogant and maybe even heretical! But every genuine Christian is *already* a move of God, a supernatural force. We are not called to be a light; it has been declared that we *are* the light—the light of Christ shining into the darkness of this world.

There is power in the blood, the blood of Christ that flows through your veins. So, wake up my fellow Christ-followers! You *are* a move of God!

ABOUT GENE BAILEY

Dr. Gene Bailey is passionate about one thing; that others come to know who Jesus is and experience the Holy Spirit gifts and manifestations in their own lives. He is the host of the television program *Revival Radio TV* that is seen around the world. Gene is sought after as a speaker and an expert on revival. Gene Bailey also serves as Senior Executive Pastor at Eagle Mountain Church in Newark, Texas. He is married to Teri and together they have seven children and reside in Aurora, Texas

Chapter 16

THE YEAR OF PERFECT VISION AND 11 DISTINCTIVES OF THE NEXT MOVE OF GOD

Kevin L. Zadai

When seeking the Lord concerning the year 2020 and beyond, I was excited to hear the Lord say to me that the coming year is "20/20, *the Year of Perfect Vision!*" The Lord is proclaiming this statement over the Body of Christ right now. He began to talk to me concerning the ability of the Holy Spirit to give us spiritual discernment to see clearly in these last days. I was reminded of the prayer that the apostle Paul prayed for the church at Ephesus:

> *Therefore I also, after I heard of your faith in the Lord Jesus and your love for all the saints, do not cease to give thanks for you, making mention of you in my prayers: that the God of our Lord Jesus Christ, the Father of glory, may give to you the spirit of wisdom and revelation in the knowledge of Him, the eyes of your understanding being enlightened; that you may know what is the hope of His calling, what are the riches of the glory of His inheritance in the saints, and what is the exceeding greatness of His power toward us who believe, according to the working of His mighty power which He worked in Christ when He raised Him from the dead and seated Him at His right hand in the heavenly places, far above all principality and power and might and dominion, and every name that is named, not only in this age but also in that which is to come. And He put all things under His feet, and gave Him to be head over all things to the church, which is His body, the fullness of Him who fills all in all* (Ephesians 1:15-23 NKJV).

Because of the Lord's desire for the believer's spiritual eyesight to be developed, we need to pray this prayer as often as possible. Personally, I pray this prayer every day and have seen my level of spiritual insight and revelation increase exponentially. The Lord wants us *to wait* in His glorious Presence for revelation that will flood us with understanding.

WAITING ON GOD

Not long ago as I was waking up in my bedroom, I saw an angel that was standing across the room by the dresser. He was dressed differently than I have ever seen an angel dressed before that time. He stood before me clothed in a very ornamented robe. It seemed as though he was waiting for me to wake up as he stood there. We were immediately caught up in the spirit. The angel took me to a specific place because he wanted to show me the secret of *waiting on God*.

I was shown the future. What I saw concerned the move of God that is coming to the earth. It was a move of the glory of the Father that saturated the atmosphere in the churches where I would be sent to preach. The angel told me that the time that I spend waiting on God will be in relation to the amount of the glory that I will be able to access in the ministry of the Holy Spirit. The angel was given permission to show me all these things so that I would be encouraged to *wait upon the Lord*. This possibility of being able to access a great amount of glory was going to be available in all the churches where I would go. I was shown churches where I had not yet even ministered. The Lord showed me that the glory was on the earth. He said Christians can enter into the glory by waiting upon Him.

Then, the angel took me into a room. Jesus was standing in that room waiting for us. Jesus seemed sad because He said, "My people were not waiting upon Me." He wanted to teach me how important it is to wait in the presence of the Lord. I realized that when I wait upon the Lord, the glory will begin to increase in my life and ministry. Next, the door through which we had just walked closed. The space that we occupied became an elevator.

Within the space, there were buttons to display the different levels of revelation that we could attain as we waited upon the Lord. The space was actually a *room of waiting*. I asked Jesus which floor I should choose, and He said that the floor that I chose was up to me. He asked me, "How long do you want to wait upon Me?" He bowed His head, and so did the angel. I bowed my head, and we waited. I felt the whole room start to ascend into the glory realm. After a while, I looked up. The elevator stopped climbing, and the door opened. We had ascended to a very high place. The room was full of revelation knowledge and glory of God.

As I looked out the door, I was looking down and seeing my life as God sees it. We had gone so high that all the things that troubled me were so small. This was the result of waiting on God. Jesus had taken me to His vantage point. It was a much better perspective of my life than I had previously known before I waited upon Him in the room of revelation.

Every Christian must receive Heaven's perspective for his or her life. This angel was given permission to show me that it is exceedingly important to wait upon God. The amount of time that a Christian is willing to wait upon the Lord is directly related to the amount of the glory that God will reveal in this generation.

> *So the Lord must wait for you to come to him so he can show you his love and compassion. For the Lord is a faithful God. Blessed are those who wait for his help* (Isaiah 30:18 NLT).

The Heavenly Key

The move of God is under way in this generation. The key is to not forcefully pursue His revelation and glory by soulish manipulation. The key here is to *wait upon the Lord*. He will cause a great and mighty flow of the glory of Father God. There are many things that must be revealed to every Christian so that they are able to understand the specific and unique ministry that God has given to them as a believer. It is especially important at this time in history for each Christian to wait upon the Lord. The angels have been assigned to every Christian to make sure that each one can receive all the briefings from Heaven that are needed in this time for this generation. I know that each believer desires to be faithful to God. Just remember, the angels of Heaven are assigned to each believer, and their desire is for each us to be faithful to God as well. Angels are trained agents of faithfulness. They cannot be denied if a Christian will continue trusting God and let angels do their job.

Believers are chosen as beloved children who have a destiny and a bright future. Every believer needs to grasp, by the Spirit's revelation, who they are to Father God. As believers, we have walked into an amazing encounter with the Spirit of God. This move of God is of historical proportions and is just ahead of us. Here are some characteristics that are very important to know concerning this epic move of God that has begun:

1. *This next move of God is the Father revealing Himself through habitation.*

We have encountered His visitation and the Spirit of revelation. When these have come into full manifestation, we will encounter the fullness of the Father's glory, which is God's habitation. In the final phase, God will not only visit us but will decide to stay with us in full manifestation as mighty miracles occur because of Father God's glory.

2. *This next move of God will involve His children beginning to understand the activity of waiting on the Lord God our Father in His Glory!*

As I have mentioned previously, there cannot be an over-emphasis on the activity of waiting on the Lord in times of meditation and prayer. We need to understand God's ways of gaining insight into His Kingdom activity. As we wait on the Lord, He comes and gives us understanding. Revelation of the Spirit will flow as we become one with Him.

3. The glory of the Father will be revealed because of His Love.

God has always loved man. The separation that we as human beings have experienced with God is not His fault. Because of sin, man is fallen and has become rebellious toward all that is good. When God shows His love through Jesus Christ, we see how good and merciful He is. *"Or do you despise the riches of His goodness, forbearance, and longsuffering, not knowing that the goodness of God leads you to repentance?"* (Rom. 2:4 NKJV).

4. The fear of the Lord will be a common occurrence that will produce humility among believers.

The fear of the Lord is coming back to the believer's life. I was assured of this many times as the Lord is setting us up for the next move of His glory. *"The fear of the Lord is the beginning of knowledge, but fools despise wisdom and instruction"* (Prov. 1:7 NKJV). We are going to encounter His awesomeness as Moses did on the holy mountain. There are certain traits that must be demonstrated by believers in order to be prepared. Moses was a very humble man and understood the fear of the Lord. *"Now the man Moses was very meek, above all the men which were upon the face of the earth"* (Num. 12:3 KJV).

In *Strong's Concordance*, the Hebrew word for meek is #6035, עָנָו 'ânâw; or "in mind (gentle) or circumstances (needy, especially saintly): humble, lowly, meek, poor." We must guard our hearts against pride and arrogance. The fear of the Lord requires us to hate pride. *"The fear of the Lord is to hate evil; pride and arrogance and the evil way and the perverse mouth I hate"* (Prov. 8:13).

5. The Father has saved the next move (the best) for Himself.

Other moves involved the Holy Spirit and Jesus revealing the Father. This next move is the move of the Father, God. He will come into our lives in an amazing way and reveal His ways to us.

6. The glory of God is the substance of His personality.

When I encountered the throne of Heaven, I realized that God's glory contained the very essence of His person. To encounter His glory is to encounter His personality!

7. The "ways of God" are His personality.

When you think of God's ways, you must understand that His ways are considered to be His pathways. He has ways of doing things and we should find out what those are. The Holy Spirit desires to lead you into those ways. Our goal is to know the only true God. Moses knew His ways (His personality); Israel saw His acts (they were spectators) (see Ps. 103:7).

8. This last move is for God's own children—those who love Him.

The world will be a *spectator* and His true children will be *participators*. We will begin to see a separation between those who genuinely love Him and those who are not sincere. We are not just to be observers but to have active encounters. Many will come to the Lord because we are participators.

9. Children will begin to take the forefront in ministry.

I also saw children being raised up with powerful ministries, starting at a young age. Get ready for them to come to the forefront.

10. Angel visitation will become common. Angels are implementors of the Father's revelation of glory.

Get ready for the holy ones to minister for you in powerful ways. They are sent to minister for you who are to "inherit salvation" (see Heb. 1:14).

11. Joy and prophesying will be accompanied with drunkenness of the Holy Spirit as people worship together everywhere.

The apostle Peter had to explain to the people that those who had the Holy Spirit fall on them were not physically drunk. Joy and prophesying are beginning to occur as believers gathers together and worship in the glory!

The future is full of the glory of God as we yield to our heavenly destinies. God has written many wonderful things in our books in Heaven for us to encounter. Soon, we will see Jesus coming in all His glory and your life down here will certainly be worth it all.

> *You saw who you created me to be before I became me!*
> *Before I'd ever seen the light of day, the number of days*
> *you planned for me were already recorded in your book*
> (Psalm 139:16 TPT).

ABOUT DR. KEVIN L. ZADAI

Kevin Zadai, ThD is dedicated to training Christians to live and operate in two realms at once—the supernatural and the natural. Called to ministry at age 10, he attended Central Bible College in Springfield, Missouri, where he received a bachelor's degree in theology. Later, Kevin received training in missions at Rhema Bible College. At age 31, during a routine surgery, he found himself on the "other side of the veil" with Jesus in a heavenly visitation that forever marked his life. This encounter ushered his ministry into new dimensions of power, activation, and impartation. Kevin is retired after being employed by Southwest Airlines for 29 years; he and his wife, Kathi, reside in New Orleans, Louisiana, and are ordained by Dr. Jesse and Dr. Cathy Duplantis.

Chapter 17

Intimacy with God, Divine Alignments, and Fruitfulness

Rev. Betty King

Dear Saints,

It is a pleasure to share with you the word of the Lord for 2020. It really is a new era, and those who understand the keys to the season will find themselves gaining strategic momentum. It is a time for divine allocation, relocation, and repositioning! I want to share these keys with you so that you can be truly fruitful this year and enter into the greater things that He has planned for you.

Rebekah's Keys to Fruitfulness

In Genesis 24, Abraham calls his oldest servant and brings him into a place of intimacy with him to give him responsibility for finding a place of alignment for his son. The servant makes an oath to Abraham there and takes precious gifts with him as he goes out to find a wife for Isaac. When the servant eventually sees Rebekah, he seeks God regarding her and looks for a confirming sign known only to himself and God. Rebekah fulfils the sign by not only refreshing him with water but his camel also. The servant then recognizes her as the one he was sent for and makes the decision to carry her back to be Isaac's wife.

However, when Isaac and Rebekah are finally married, she struggles with fertility issues as Abraham's wife had a generation before. Although the servant had chosen the right woman for Isaac, the cycle of barrenness was not immediately broken. It was only lifted eventually through Isaac's prayers.

As I was interceding before the Lord for the Body of Christ, He brought this passage and all its components to mind. In 2020, there are many keys that must come together to bring about the fruitfulness He has intended for us.

Intimacy with the Father

First, Abraham's servant took an oath in a place of intimacy. This was the only place from which he could truly understand the heart of his master. Coming out of that exchange, there was no way that he would take a decision lightly regarding Isaac's future. It is only from the place of intimacy that God can entrust us to responsibly carry out the weighty matters of His heart and make the decisions that are right for His Son and preserve the purity of His will. We must prioritize entering into that place with Him throughout this year. What we learn and receive from Him there will be key to the fruitfulness of future generations of the Church. His plans for His Church must be handled carefully, and we need His heart to show us how.

Finding Alignments that Restore and Refresh

Second, Rebekah refreshed both the servant and the vehicle that had carried him to her. In that moment of refreshing, the servant was assured that he was making the right decision and both he and his vehicle were made ready for the next stage of the journey. In the coming together of right relationships and alignments there will be a sense of refreshing not only for the individuals involved but also for those who support them, providing them with energy and strength for the road ahead. We must be careful to recognize and honor those relationships that produce life in us and those we do life with. These alignments will release the vitality needed to take our next steps and gain momentum in 2020.

Persistence and Prayer

Sarah was barren for many years in her marriage to Abraham, and in the next generation Rebekah faced the same issue. Shadows of the past and the memories of hardship within the family could easily have become discouragements. In the Body of Christ today there are various instances of replacement theology circulating, wherein old wounds and unresolved cycles have caused some people to voice opinions that play down the power and truth of God for His Church today. God's power does not diminish with time, and in 2020 it will still be by pure trust in God that His people overcome their circumstances. He is still able to break in and break through, according to His sovereignty and not based on the limitations of our individual perceptions.

Then there was the power of prayer that finally lifted the curse. Even when the signs have been given and the right relationships have come together, prayer remains at the heart of fulfilling destiny. What has started with God must be brought back before Him for increase and fruitfulness. The house of God in 2020 must still be a house of prayer! When all the components of intimacy, alignment, persistence, and prayer come together, there will be fruit that changes nations. The Lord is ready to partner with His church to see revival!

His Presence Is a Key to the Greater Things

When He appointed them into the Great Commission, Jesus declared to His disciples *"Behold, I am with you always"* (Matt. 28:20). While I was before the Lord, this statement dropped into my spirit. I have always been very much aware of this promise in my walk with God, and for me it is one of the most powerful in the Word. It is a wonder to know that our Father and the One we serve in Heaven has made this commitment to us! The promise also contains keys that we need for the year ahead.

Knowing What It Means for Him to Be Close

Jesus' promise does not mean that we won't face issues or challenges. What it does mean, however, is that His Presence is always nearby and that He is always available to us. When we are alive to this promise, we are able to be continuously aware of His Presence and protection throughout the day and bring Him into all that we do. When we know that He is near, the emotions that have kept many from pursuing the higher calling are put to one side. True momentum in 2020 will not come from thinking that there will not be obstacles but will come by facing them head on with the One who is with us!

Knowing He Is Near Elevates Us Even Through Trials

Joseph saw God's plan for his life through dreams but had to pass through many trials while he learned to steward His promises in the face of jealousy, envy, and setbacks. What really blesses me about Joseph's life is that his mind was always clearly stayed on God and he was always conscious of His Presence, no matter what was going on. When Potiphar's wife tried to seduce him, the Presence of God caused him to flee from compromise regardless of the emotional pressures of being a slave. In prison, God was still able to communicate with him and he was able to do God's will, helping others by interpreting their dreams. This ability to be conscious of God at all times is a key to the greater things, and when Joseph finally left the prison, he left to rule a nation. In 2020, cultivating your awareness of God during times of challenge will prepare you for strategic elevation.

STRATEGIC KEYS FOR THE GOVERNMENTAL ANOINTING

Daniel was another person who experienced strategic elevation in the midst of trials because he truly understood the keys to his situation. He had been brought to Babylon as a captive at a young age. In the midst of the intimidation and threats, and despite the emotional pressures that came with losing his home and comforts, he found a strategy and wisdom in God that allowed him to prosper and appear before kings with true prophetic authority. In 2020, God is seeking to increase the governmental anointing on His Body and will cause it to rest on those who embrace the keys that made Daniel's life such a powerful witness.

Honor That Shifts Strongholds

As a young person in Babylon, Daniel experienced many things that could have caused him to take offence and he would have seen many people defile themselves with the temptations of the environment. Yet he fought to keep his heart pure, not only toward God but also toward those over him and around him in every situation. He honored people despite their compromise and animosity and even interceded to save the lives of those he could have treated as enemies. This relentless honor shifted strongholds in the system and brought him before the king where his gift could have its greatest impact. In all of this, even in the times of his greatest success, he also never forgot to honor the city of Jerusalem and the nation from which he had come.

As I prayed, I saw a younger generation arising, anointed to move in honor toward those over and around them and so bring healing and influence into the Church. Because they honored those over them and around them so well, they carried a measure of glory that enabled them to shift the strongholds of offence between generations and between different streams within the Church. I saw them go out from honored leaders as sent ones into places and situations where rebellion had flourished through misunderstanding and mispresentation, and intercept pollution and negativity, refusing to let it go any further. I saw them bringing healing to many fathers of the Church whose hope for the next generation had begun to waver, strengthening these fathers to bring life to other sons and daughters whose hearts had gone far from God. They lived as shields of the earth, preserving the pure things of God through loyalty and consistency, working with the true fathers and mothers in the Body, shifting strongholds in every sphere of influence, and moving in great financial and governmental breakthrough.

Be encouraged pastors, leaders, and pioneers. God is stirring the winds of revival! The fresh release of honor will address issues that have arisen because of false liberty, mixture, and compromise. Keep standing in the gate! God will reward you for the sacrifices you have made for the next generation, and in the coming season of honor the sheep that you have cared for will bless you and your families.

Governmental Alignment That Preserves

A time came when Daniel faced execution in the lion's den. His very life had been sought for by people who were jealous of him and considered him an obstacle to their ambitions. However, although a decree had been made against his life according to law, and although he had been placed in the pit with the lions for execution, no harm came to him. His key was walking in governmental alignment. His enemies had set up a situation that called for him to be judged, but real authority for judgement belonged to God and the king, who both knew Daniel's innocence because he walked with them and had aligned his heart with theirs.

As I was praying for church leadership to be strengthened and refreshed, I saw the Lord pouring balm on the wounds of those He has called and speaking tenderly to them. Like Daniel, no weapon formed against you shall prosper! If He has called you, He will protect you. Only be careful not to do anything in your own strength and to walk in alignment with governmental authority in Heaven and on earth.

THE SPIRIT OF THE LORD IS ON YOU

Isaiah 61 says the Spirit of the Lord is on us. In this new era the presence of God is so important. Remember His promises, that He is with us, and what you are able to do by the Spirit of God that is on you. I pray for you to have the full understanding of this and the confidence that comes with it. Don't let the compromising thoughts of others be projected onto you. Pull such things down quickly.

2020 is such a strategic year of promise. I pray that God will help you to use these keys to unlock the treasures He has written into His book for you.

Gripped by His love,
Rev. Betty King

ABOUT BETTY KING

Reverend King has been a minister of the gospel for more than 27 years & Betty King International Ministries (BKIM) was founded in 1998 as a prayer and intercession ministry for people who were in need. It is a conduit to see people permanently delivered from their trials and afflictions. BKIM is a dynamically prophetic hub of prayer and revival that continues to touch many lives and nations with the love and power of God. Through various ministries they provide socio-economic and spiritual solutions to cause fruitfulness in every area of life!

Chapter 18

A TIME OF GENERATIONAL PROPHETIC INHERITANCE

James W. Goll

Often at the head of the New Year, in both the Hebrew calendar and the civil calendar, the Holy Spirit speaks concerning things to come. As I have prayed and sought the face of God, I have been given a series of revelations concerning the New Era we have now entered into of 5780 corresponding to the year of 2020 and beyond. We are not just crossing from one year to the next, but from one era or decade to the next in this strategic period of time.

We really are crossing over from one side of the river where promises are revealed to the other side where promises are manifested. Could it be that we are in a season that is described in Joshua 4? On one side of the river there were great prophetic revelations received and released. Then there came a crossing over moment. The priestly leaders led the way, and in the process they were instructed to pick up stones and deposit them on the other side of the Jordan. This pile of stones became "memorial stones" speaking to the generations to come of their inherited prophetic promises.

Moses had released amazing prophetic revelations that apparently had a long shelf life. What do I mean by that phrase? The revelation that the "meekest man" that ever walked the face of the earth was given did not find immediate fulfilment. They were generational prophetic words. They were passed down from one generation to the next.

Passing of the Baton

Let me bring us up to date and to another period of time where the baton is being passed from one generation to the next. The modern prophetic movement finds its birth in the year of 1988. The "naba" and the "seer" streams of the prophetic anointing came forth with a burst of excitement in 1948. Two divergent streams appeared on the scene of time in the form of the Healing Deliverance Movement and the Latter Rain Outpouring. These were two entirely different operations of the Holy Spirit, but each had a major impact in the Body of Christ in a global manner.

Then one generation later these two expressions reemerged in 1988. Bishop Bill Hamon of Christian International became one of the primary fathers of the spontaneous, effervescent "naba prophetic" flow where he eventually established a base in the pan handle of Florida. Paul Cain and Bob Jones, on the other hand, were recognized by many as some of the significant forerunners of the "seer prophets" based out of Kansas City. John Paul Jackson, myself, and others became identified as a part of the historic "Kansas City Prophets" in the late 1980s and early 1990s. Two streams. Two different operations. Two different generations. The baton was being passed on from one generation to the next. Great promises. Great problems. Great inheritance.

Thirty-two years have already come and gone since these two historic streams of the prophetic found their rebirth into prominence on a global scene. Today we have the benefit of cross pollination, the joining of the generations, the inclusion of numerous highly gifted women in the prophetic, and an entire new generation of emerging prophets on an international level.

Today we have prophetic intercessors, prophetic evangelists, revelatory teachers, anointed counsellors, strategic marketplace prophets, prophetic equippers, dream interpreters, apostolic prophets, revelatory administrators and pastors, hope solutionists, and entrepreneurs and prophetic consultants in all of the seven spheres of culture. It is an entire new era. We have crossed over from promise revealed to promise fulfilled.

The Body of Christ has never seen this level of prophetic profusion—ever! We are in a new era. We are inheriting the promises of these trail blazing forerunners and crossing the Jordan once again to walk out the words that a previous generation declared. It is a time of manifest destiny. It is a time of generational prophetic inheritance.

WE EACH HAVE A PORTION!

We each have a strategic role to play. We each have a unique prophetic expression to release. We must take our place on the wall. It is imperative that we work together. The new wine is found in the cluster. We really are better together. It is no longer time to say, "The harvest is a decade away." No! It is time to receive your prophetic inheritance and walk it out for Jesus Christ's sake! It is time to put in the sickle for the harvest is indeed ripe.

You have a voice that needs to be heard. It is a voice that cries in the wilderness, "Make way for the Kingdom of God!" Our voices together exemplify the sound of many rushing waters. The voice of the Lord is thundering once again. Will your piercing trumpet sound be heard? Will you be a part of the symphonic sound that the world is waiting to hear? The choice is yours to make.

It's a new song for a new era. We each have a particular line in Heaven's song to sing to a hurting world. The earth is groaning to sing this song of faith, hope, and love. We must each lean into our Master's heart and listen to the now voice of the Holy Spirit. You are to be a voice in the earth and not just an echo. We each have a voice that needs to be heard. And this I know, after four failed attempts of dying, I have a voice that needs to be heard in this pivotal hour.

Proclaim for All to Hear

I agree with so many others that we are shifting from an emphasis of the "Year of the Eye" to the "Year of the Mouth." But because my expertise is not in Hebrew numeric interpretation, I feel I must stay in my lane of prophetic teaching, supernatural encounters, and inspirational revelations. With that in mind, let me give you the distinctions I have been granted in recent weeks and months. I have chosen to frame my portion as eight prophetic proclamations.

We do not use the words "proclaim" or "proclamation" often in our ordinary speech. We prefer the synonymous words such as "announce" or "publish" or "invite" or "declare." Let's revive *proclamation* as one of our best ways of being prophetic in these days. Let's "cry out," "pronounce," "herald," or even "decree."

Let me give you two primary scripture references on this subject.

> *I will proclaim the name of Lord. Oh, praise the greatness of our God! He is the Rock, his works are perfect, and all his ways are just. A faithful God who does no wrong, upright and just is He* (Deuteronomy 32:3-4 NIV).

> *What I tell you in the darkness, speak in the light; and what you hear whispered in your ear, proclaim upon the housetops* (Matthew 10:27 NASB).

This principle was driven home to me one day when I was alone, waiting quietly upon the Lord, and the voice of the Holy Spirit came to me saying, *"It is time to make a worldwide impact by calling forth the watchmen to the prophetic power of proclamation."* This additional piece of the puzzle has shifted me into ministering out of a higher vision. Let's release greater impact through the prophetic power of proclamation.

Eight Prophetic Proclamations

1. It is a time of a fresh restoration of righteousness.

This deals with the realization that righteousness is both a gift and an out working in our lifestyle and character. This movement will be based in part out of Psalm 24:3-4: "Who can ascend to the hill of the Lord? But he who has clean hands and a pure heart." It will be a time when "the Spirit comes with conviction."

2. It is a time of divine interruptions.

God is going to interrupt our schedules, our meetings, and our appointments with His presence. The Holy Spirit is going to interrupt our good program-based agendas with interruptions of His divine presence. Watch out, here comes God as the Divine Interrupter and Divine Intruder!

3. It is a time when divine order will be established.

Out of a season when there is the open conflict of thrones resulting in chaos and confusion, the enemy will over-play his hand. God will use this backdrop to have the final word. This has ramifications on many fronts from family to government.

4. It is a time of sacred assemblies and consecration.

Out of need, there will be a movement of unity where there will be city-wide, state or provincial, and national gatherings to seek the face of the Lord. There will be more public rallies of repentance and prayer combined with the call to *"go* therefore" over the next three years and beyond than in any previous time in church history.

5. It is a time of cleansing of old disappointments.

We cannot carry this baggage into the new era. Therefore, the Holy Spirit is initiating a movement of cleansing from old disappointments so that we can come into the new with a fresh slate without remorse, guilt, and shame so that we can be the hope ambassadors He intends.

6. It is a time when the thief and the robber are exposed and caught.

I have been given dreams where a security breach has occurred and been exposed. Two dark demonic entities then came and appeared before me and their names were "thief and robber." These enemies will be exposed and captured. Then the voice of the Lord came to me saying, *"It is time for my revolutionary midnight riders to appear of the scene. They will shine the light in darkness and expose the deeds of darkness."*

7. It is a time when there is revelatory teaching on power and authority.

As a part of our equipment needed for the new era, the Holy Spirit will be teaching us on the difference between power and authority and the necessity for both. There will be a revisiting of the themes of the authority of the believer in Christ Jesus.

8. It is a time for the beginning of the great harvest.

This new era in Christendom is the beginning of the great harvest. Please note, I did not say the final harvest. But we are crossing the threshold into the greatest harvest we have ever known thus far. It is time for the "greatest show on Earth" of signs and wonders and open displays of God's lavish love when Jesus Christ receives the reward for His suffering.

THREE REQUIREMENTS ARE NECESSARY

Let me close my portion of this compilation by giving you three simple requirements that are necessary to walk in this new era of divine destiny and to see these eight prophetic proclamations come to fulfillment. The requirements are simple and yet quite profound. It is a time for:

1.   Greater Focus

2.   Greater Flexibility

3.   Greater Wholeness

I trust this exhortation has stirred your faith and helped to bring you to higher vision where each heart and voice matters. Yes, we each see in part and know in part. But when we each bring our part to the table together, we see the greater whole. So this is a portion of what I see, hear, and know for the new Hebrew year of 5780 and the new civil year of 2020 and beyond!

Let's each receive and walk out our portion of this generational prophetic inheritance. Let's each volunteer freely in this time when His manifested power and glory are on display. I want to see Jesus Christ receive the reward of His suffering. Don't you?

Yes, it is a new era in church history. It is time to fulfill generational prophetic promises. It's time for the "greatest show on Earth" to begin!

With anticipation,
JAMES W. GOLL

ABOUT JAMES W. GOLL

James W. Goll is the co-founder of God Encounters Ministries—a ministry to the nations. He is the author of over twenty-five books and study guides, including *The Seer, Dream Language,* and *The Lifestyle of a Prophet.* James is a member of the Harvest International Ministries Apostolic Team, the Apostolic Council of Prophetic Elders, and other national and international ministries. James continues to write, travel the globe preaching and ministering and lives in the beautiful hills of Franklin, Tennessee.

Chapter 19

A VISION OF THE UNIFIED CHURCH AND THE THIRD MISSING MOVE OF GOD

Larry Sparks

Unity is key right now. In the earlier prophetic observation, I noted there is a very vicious and intentional attack right now aimed at unity among believers. Why? Satan fears any manifestation of John 17. Jesus envisioned a unified company of people functioning *as one* even as He, the Father, and the Spirit are One. It would be through a unified church or ecclesia that the glory of Jesus would be revealed to the world. And it would be *by this* the world would indeed know and believe that God had sent Jesus to the Earth (see John 17:21). *Shocking.* We cannot underestimate the importance and power of believers dwelling together in unity, moving toward one shared, common goal.

I want to share this vision, as I believe it will give some uncomfortable (but very encouraging) context to where the Lord desires to take things. This was not an "open vision," where I literally saw this play out before my physical eyes. This has been more of a "vision in progress," where snapshots of this scene have popped into my mind over a period of time. Then, during times of ministering prophetically, I would see it with greater clarity.

Just be aware, anytime I share this vision I sense that I am pushing against something in the spirit realm. What is it? Some demonic principality or stronghold of thought that insists what is presented in this vision could *never happen* because these two realities *do not belong together.* Whenever you begin to prophesy something and are immediately hit with thoughts that say "don't even say this because that could *never* happen," there is a chance you are confronting some high-level principality or stronghold of thought that, until you decided to prophesy against it, has remained uncontested and unchallenged. Prophetic words (when accurate and spoken first by the voice of the Lord) actually confront strongholds of thought that have never been challenged. You will even begin to feel the discomfort of the demonic realm when you introduce new Kingdom thoughts and paradigms into the equation, for until you opened your mouth and released Holy Spirit utterance, that demonic stronghold had "run of the place." Now, a Kingdom decree has been released. When the people of God both pray and practice the prophetic words that are released, the forces of hell don't stand a chance!

A Sanctuary of Sound Doctrine... and Supernatural Encounter

In this vision, I saw a church sanctuary, very similar to Pastor Alistair Begg's Parkside Church in Cleveland, Ohio. If you are unfamiliar with Pastor Begg, I would enthusiastically encourage you to check out his wonderful expository, Bible-based and Christ-centered teaching materials available through his ministry, *Truth for Life*. This is truly the "meat" of the Word. Pastor Begg is definitely more reformed in his theological persuasion—which is fine by me! We may disagree on some "non-essential" items, but at the day's end I truly feast on the amazing teaching he brings to the table (and the amazing Scottish accent amplifies it all the more!).

Back to the vision. I saw a sanctuary similar to Begg's, with a pastor ministering from the pulpit just like him. Whether it was Alistair Begg or not, I could not be sure. I just knew the preacher's cadence and content was very similar to Begg's in that he was delivering a solid exposition of Scripture. It was not a "hip" or "cool" type of church. There was something timeless about it, something majestic, something reverent.

But then, at the same time, I saw the altar area. People were radically being touched by the presence and power of the Holy Spirit. Some were weeping; some were laughing. Some were on their backs; some on their faces. Some were shaking; some were sitting in silence. There was all manner of holy chaos taking place at the altar, while the preacher continued to deliver a solid expository message to an attentive, on-looking congregation (not distracted by the phenomena at the altar). This vision presents two realities that should be incompatible. The devil would love us to continue to believe they will not operate together, solid exposition of the Scriptures and a radical move of the Spirit, but I believe it's not only possible, but it's what will become normative for those who would say "Yes" to the Spirit's movement in the days ahead.

Why is this environment so important? Upper rooms are wombs that ignite movements and birth souls. The church must arise and become the global upper room it was always meant to be—yes, a place of teaching and preaching, but also a place of Holy Spirit encounter and commissioning. More about this to come, as I endeavor to tie this all in together. It's this kind of church that will be instrumental is stepping *beyond* another Jesus People Movement and bringing us into a true reformation of culture.

We Don't Need Another Jesus People Movement; We Need a Jesus Reformation

Even though I mentioned part of this prophetic word in the *Prophetic Words for 2019* volume, I cannot escape its relevance for right now. So I conclude with this vision of where, I believe, the Lord desires to take us in the days ahead.

Many are crying out for another Jesus People Movement. Their intentions are pure and noble, but I've got to be honest—I don't want another Jesus People Movement unless it comes with a moral and cultural reformation.

In the 1960s and 1970s, I believe we were meant to experience three unique phases of transformation; we hit two quite successfully, but missed the third. Allow me to briefly explain, as I believe history gives us a prophetic pattern for how to prepare for something that is coming—yes, I believe that something is "at hand." The question is, *are we ready to venture into something new, unfamiliar, and uncomfortable or will we default into what's comfortable, familiar, and successful* (according to natural human guidelines)?

THE CHARISMATIC RENEWAL OF THE 1960S

Up until the 1960s, the experience of Holy Spirit baptism and the fullness of Pentecostal power was widely reserved—more or less—to the Pentecostal denominations, most of which were birthed from the 1906 Azusa Street Revival. But as we all know, you cannot keep the Holy Spirit contained. Just as God would not allow Himself to be contained in a "box" for long (the Ark of the Covenant), so the Spirit was brooding in a mighty way in the 1960s, setting the whole planet up for an outstanding renewal.

During this period, no mainline denomination was safe from an "Upper Room" encounter with the Holy Spirit. Presbyterians, Methodists, Baptists, Lutherans—these traditional protestant denominations all, to some degree or another, experienced a fresh baptism of the Holy Spirit. Different leaders and churches in these denominations were being touched by God afresh. Many consider the key catalyst to the Charismatic Renewal being Dennis Bennett, an Episcopalian priest who was filled with the Holy Spirit, spoke in tongues, and became a testimony of what's possible for all believers (Pentecostal or not). If Bennett could experience such a powerful baptism of the Holy Spirit, surely every believer had access! Truly, the Pentecostal paradigm was being powerfully confronted with the many unique denominations being impacted by this landscape-sweeping renewal. One of the strongest movements to emerge from this period was the Catholic Charismatic Renewal, which still has powerful impact and influence to this very day.

Bottom line: in the 1960s, the church experienced a corporate "Upper Room" outpouring that renewed and refreshed the Body of Christ.

THE JESUS PEOPLE MOVEMENT OF THE '60S AND '70S

On the heels of the Charismatic Renewal, you had the Jesus People Movement. In many ways, these movements took place concurrently. Many date the beginning of the Charismatic movement to be April 3, 1960, when Dennis Bennett shared his Spirit-baptism experienced with his church, St. Mark's Episcopal Church in Van Nuys, California.

As for the Jesus People Movement, it's a bit harder to pinpoint an exact start date or specific catalyst that launched it; however, many would argue that it began in the late 1960s, early 1970s. If the 1960s was a period of renewal in the Church, I believe the late '60s and '70s, with the Jesus People Movement, was a revival. Renewal refreshed the church, while revival brought the unchurched and unsaved in to the Kingdom of God.

During this time, "make love, not war" was the mantra of the age, hippy culture was flourishing, and drugs were claiming the minds (and lives) of a generation. In the midst of the rampant sin, rebellion, and immorality, one could clearly see that an entire generation was desperate for *something*. What happened? I believe it was an Isaiah 6/Acts 2 moment.

In Isaiah 6, the prophet Isaiah encounters God in a powerful, life-altering way. This reminds me that great commissions are launched with great encounters. We don't wake up one morning with the bright idea to go and change the world; we receive the call to be "sent ones" in those tenderizing moments in the fiery presence of God. This happened to Isaiah. This happened to Moses at the burning bush. This happened to John on the Isle of Patmos. This happened to the 120 in the Upper Room on the Day of Pentecost. Great commissions are birthed with great encounters.

Following Isaiah's encounter, the prophet responds to the commission of Heaven where God asks: *"Whom shall I send, and who will go for us?"* (Isa. 6:8). Often, a sign that the Lord is seeking a "sent one" is the desperate cry of a generation. Remember the cry of the Israelites under Egyptian bondage. Their cry ascended to Heaven, and what was God's response? Moses. Throughout history, we witness this cycle repeating itself. People would cry out and God would often answer that cry with a reformer, with a redeemer, with a prophet, with a judge, with a king, with a leader, with a Kingdom solutionist. God typically answers a cry by commissioning a "sent one." The Spirit-empowered, Spirit-renewed church of the 1960s was the "sent one" messenger to reach and help rescue the lost ones of the late '60s and '70s.

THE CHILDREN OF RENEWAL: SOULS

I'm convinced that the Jesus People Movement of the 1970s was the offspring of the Upper Room that was established in the 1960s during the Charismatic Renewal. What God did through a Spirit-filled ecclesia (church community) in the 1960s became a womb to birthing the millions of souls that came into the Kingdom of God during the Jesus People Movement. Remember, we don't evaluate the legitimacy of Upper Rooms by manifestations or unusual spiritual phenomena. What do I mean? Obviously, there is the Upper Room in Acts 2 where the Spirit descended on the Day of Pentecost. That is the definitive "Upper Room" experience. However, as we look throughout history, we see Upper Room places, times, and seasons, where it seems that God pours out His Spirit in a powerful, unusual manner. These periods are often referred to as times of renewal and awakening.

On the Day of Pentecost, the Holy Spirit's coming was accompanied by an array of unusual phenomena—a supernatural sound, a mighty rushing wind, tongues of fire, and the miraculous ability to communicate the wonders of God to diverse people groups spanning different languages (see Acts 2:1-4). Pentecost was unusual to say the least. How did the onlooking public respond to this outpouring? Take note, they were "bewildered" (v. 6), "amazed and astonished" (v. 7), "amazed and perplexed" (v. 12) and mocking, claiming those filled with the Spirit were "filled with new wine" (v. 13—which was quite true!). The point is this: we don't evaluate the success of Pentecost based on what some "devout" people thought (v. 5). I mention the word "devout" because it sounds like the multitude of those present were religious in some capacity. I'm sure that one of the reasons people mocked the disciples and claimed they were drunk is because that measure of Holy Spirit outpouring confronted their religious paradigm. Either way, the telltale signs of Pentecost's success were the birth of the New Testament church, the fulfilment of Jesus' promise to send the Holy Spirit, and of course the conversion of at least 3,000 souls on that day (v. 41).

Likewise, the telltale sign of the Charismatic Renewal's impact was the birth of the Jesus People Movement. I have no doubt these two movements are joined at the hip in the spirit, with the first being a renewal of believers and the second being a revival that brings the lost into the Kingdom of God.

It's Time for the "Missing Third Move"

At the beginning of this explanation, I mentioned "three movements" that were meant to take place in the 1960s and '70s. We saw two historical spiritual movements, but I believe we stopped short of the third, which was meant to produce a reformation.

- Charismatic Renewal: renewal and refreshing of the church through the power of the Holy Spirit.

- Jesus People Movement: revival in the church impacts the lost and sees millions brought into the Kingdom of God.

I believe the devil entered the equation and strategically hijacked the reformation that should have taken place. He could not stop the momentum of renewal and revival, so he short circuited the possibility for societal reformation. Why is this important?

What *could* have happened is the redeemed souls of the Jesus People Movement decided to translate their zeal and passion for Christ through societal integration and impact. In other words, those who got saved during the Jesus People Movement become influencers in every sphere of society, bringing Kingdom impact to arts and entertainment, government, business, media, family, education, and the church. This did *not* happen. Why?

We believed we were living in a "late great planet Earth." The dismal eschatological narrative (end-time theology) of the day was "buckle up and get ready—the rapture of the church is happening at any moment and you don't want to defile yourself by being involved with areas of society and culture that are doomed to be destroyed by the anti-Christ and wrath of God." That's my interpretation anyway. This is not an attack against rapture theology; far from it. There are many who believe that Jesus will supernaturally remove Christians from the Earth in an event called the *Rapture of Church*, just prior to seven years of great tribulation being unleashed upon the Earth— and yet, these people believe that until that happens, we have a commission to be transformational Kingdom influencers. The issue of the '60s and '70s is really a timeless problem that Jesus prophetically addressed in the Gospels. It's the concealing of our lights under a bushel. Pay close attention to Jesus' language in His classic discussion of being "salt and light."

> *You are the salt of the earth. But what good is salt if it has lost its flavor? Can you make it salty again? It will be thrown out and trampled underfoot as worthless.*
>
> *You are the light of the world—like a city on a hilltop that cannot be hidden. No one lights a lamp and then puts it under a basket. Instead, a lamp is placed on a stand, where it gives light to everyone in the house. In the same way, let your good deeds shine out for all to see, so that everyone will praise your heavenly Father* (Matthew 5:13-16 NLT).

You are the salt of the—what? *The Earth.* Not salt of the church or Christian community. Your saltiness, your life, is meant to have a flavoring impact on the world around you. If not, there is a rebuke waiting: "It will be thrown out and trampled underfoot as worthless." I propose to you that a Christian faith that has no measurable impact upon the world, society, and darkness around it is worthless and will be trampled upon.

Likewise, Jesus says we are the light of the—what? *The world.* Yes, a world that's riddled with disease and pain, war and famine, chaos and crisis. A world where entertainers and celebrities occupy the pulpits of a generation, where sin is called "culturally progressive" and the new tolerance is "accept sin or be treated as a bigot." The world is dark and often antagonistic toward the Christian faith. How will you choose to respond? We could disengage and let darkness continue to reign unchallenged and uncontested. Or, we could actually step into the reformational role that Jesus envisioned when He called us salt of the Earth and light of world. We cannot repeat the mistake of the Jesus People Movement, exalting spirituality to such a high degree that we lose our relevance to the culture around us. Yes, Jesus is returning. But I am convinced He is returning for a *return on His investment.* He's made a sizable investment in us, His church. He's given us His Spirit and I'm quite convinced that when the Son of Man returns, He will be looking for measurable signs of how a people, filled with the Holy Spirit, impacted the world around them.

ABOUT LARRY SPARKS

Larry Sparks is publisher for Destiny Image, a Spirit-filled publishing house birthed in 1983 with a mandate to *publish the prophets*. With a MDiv. in Church History and Renewal from Regent University, Larry is a prophetic minister who teaches individuals and church environments how to create space for the Holy Spirit to move in presence, prophetic utterance, and power. Larry has been featured on Sid Roth's *It's Supernatural!,* the *Jim Bakker Show,* CBN, TBN, the ElijahList, and *Charisma Magazine.* Larry is also host of *The Prophetic Edge* featured on GOD TV. He lives in Texas with his wife and daughter. For more information visit: larrysparksministries.com.

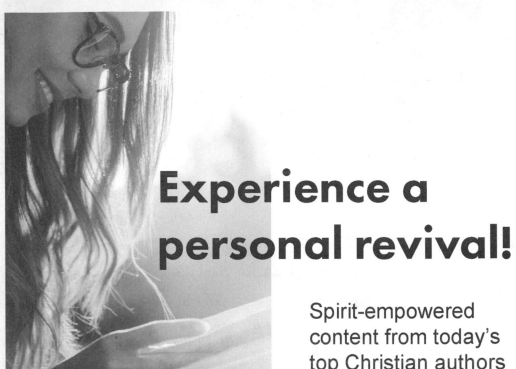